We Are Our Own Enemies

The Enemy Within

By

Daniel Meguille

© Copyright 2025 Daniel Meguille. All rights reserved.

It is illegal to reproduce, duplicate or transmit any part of this document in either electronic means or printed format. Recording of this publication is strictly prohibited.

Dedication

To my client, whose mind overflows with ideas yet too often hesitates to release them into the world, I dedicate this book. Time and again, you have brought me concepts brimming with promise—seeds that, if planted, nurtured, and tended with care, could grow into something extraordinary. And yet, many have remained unplanted, waiting for the "perfect" moment—a moment that never seems to arrive.

In you, I see not only your own struggle, but a universal one: the battle between intention and action, vision and execution.

This dedication, then, extends beyond you, my client, to all who have stood at the threshold of change with desire in their hearts but hesitation in their steps. It is for those who resolved to improve their lives—financially, physically, emotionally, or spiritually—yet stopped short of acting. For those who wrote goals in journals, drafted business plans, outlined routines, and promised themselves new beginnings, only to watch those intentions fade beneath the weight of excuses, distractions, or fear.

This book is both a mirror and a reminder. A mirror, to help you recognise the patterns that keep you stuck and to unmask self-sabotage when it disguises itself as caution, preparation, or waiting for the "right time." And a reminder, that the greatest obstacles are not out there—in the economy, in competitors, or in doubters, but within. They take the form of procrastination, fear of failure, fear of success, or the endless cycle of overthinking.

Yet let this also be a message of hope. The very fact that you dream, that you return again and again with fresh ideas, proves your spirit has not given up. You still carry the spark of possibility—and that is no small gift. The question has never been whether you are capable, but whether you are willing to act despite your doubts.

To my client, and to every reader who sees themselves in these words: may you find the courage to cross from thought into action. May you learn that perfection is not a prerequisite for progress, and that steady, imperfect steps build the foundation of remarkable achievements. May you silence the inner critic that delays your potential, and replace hesitation with boldness.

If this book does anything, let it awaken you to this truth: the real battle is not against the world, but against yourself. And once you conquer that inner struggle, little else can stand in your way.

This book is for you—the dreamers, the planners, the visionaries ready to move beyond hesitation. May it inspire you to turn vision into action, and dreams into reality.

Daniel Meguille

Contents

Preface 1
Mirror War 3
   Reflections of Truth 3
   The Façade of Identity 8
   The Path to Acceptance 14
Fear: The Silent Killer of Dreams 20
   The Roots of Fear 20
   Confronting the Shadows 25
   The Cost of Inaction 30
The Prison of Doubt 37
   Unravelling Self-Doubt 37
   Breaking Free from Chains 41
Comfort Zones and the Illusion of Safety 48
   The Fallacy of Comfort 48
   The Call to Adventure 53
   Testing Boundaries 59
Procrastination: Tomorrow's Greatest Thief 65
   The Lure of Delay 65
   Strategies for Action 70
Negative Self-Talk and the Inner Critic 78
   Voices We Inherit 78
   Rewriting the Script 84
Envy, Jealousy, and Comparison 89

    Dark Companions 89

    Cultivating Gratitude 94

    Building Compassionate Connections 100

The Fear of Success 107

    Success Paradox 107

    Redefining Success 112

    Embracing Risks 116

    Celebrating Successes, Big and Small 122

    Conclusion 123

Pride and Ego 125

    The Masks We Wear 125

    Vulnerability and Connection 131

    Healing Through Reconciliation 137

Manipulation and Control 142

    The Hidden Dynamics 142

    Recognizing Manipulation 148

    Establishing Healthy Boundaries 154

Greed: The Root of Many Evils 160

    The Allure of Greed 160

    The Cost of Excess 166

    Cultivating Contentment 172

Foreword 179

Preface

We Are Our Own Enemies is not just a phrase; it is a truth that many of us live with but often fail to confront. Life presents us with countless challenges, yet time and again I have come to realise that the most brutal battles are not fought against the world outside, but against the shadows within ourselves. Fear, doubt, insecurity, pride, procrastination, and even self-sabotage—these are the silent forces that hold us back, restraining our growth and clouding our vision of what is truly possible.

This book was born out of a deep desire to reflect on those struggles and to share insights that might help us all face them with greater courage and clarity. It is not written from a place of perfection; I am as much a traveller on this journey as you are. Instead, it is written with honesty, humility, and hope. I hope that through these words, you will recognise parts of your own journey, find encouragement in knowing you are not alone, and gather strength to rise above the inner battles that threaten to define you.

As you turn these pages, you will find a blend of storytelling, reflection, and lessons drawn from both personal experience and universal truths. This is not a book of condemnation but one of illumination. It asks us to look in the mirror, not to criticise ourselves, but to see clearly, to understand, and to move forward. True change begins the moment we accept responsibility for our part in our struggles, and even more importantly, when we choose to act differently.

I believe that words have power. They can wound, but they can also heal. They can divide, but they can also unite. They can keep us trapped in cycles of defeat, but they can also inspire us to break free and step boldly into new possibilities. It is with that conviction that I offer this book to you. My words are not magic, but perhaps they will serve as a spark—something to ignite a fire of reflection, courage, and transformation in your own life.

Reading this book is an adventure. It is a journey inward, one that might at times feel uncomfortable but will always be worth the effort. If you allow it, you will discover insights not only about the world but about yourself—the kind of insights that lead to growth, freedom, and peace.

So, here's to the adventure we are about to take together. Here's to the moments of clarity that will shine like light through the cracks of our uncertainty. Here's to the magic of words and the power they hold to remind us of who we truly are and who we are meant to become.

Let us make this journey unforgettable—one page, one thought, one breakthrough at a time.

With all my heart,
D. Meguille

Mirror War

Reflections of Truth

The journey of self-perception is complex, a mirror that reflects not just our physical selves but also the intricate tapestry of our thoughts, beliefs, and experiences. It can serve as a sanctuary or a battleground, shaping our identity and influencing how we navigate the world. In the quiet moments of introspection, we often find ourselves wrestling with the dualities within—light and shadow, strength and weakness, courage and fear. These reflections are not just personal; they are shaped by societal influences, cultural narratives, and shared experiences that can both distort and illuminate our self-image. The Seeker, a character whose journey embodies the struggle of self-discovery, often found themselves standing before their own metaphorical mirror, questioning the very essence of who they were.

There were days when that reflection radiated confidence and clarity, illuminating the path ahead. But there were also days—oh, so many days—when the person staring back seemed shrouded in dimness, burdened by the weight of expectations and self-doubt. It was during one of these tumultuous periods that The Seeker experienced a profound moment of realisation. One late afternoon, amidst the whirlwind of life, they sat alone in a park, grappling with feelings of inadequacy. As shadows lengthened and the sun dipped below the horizon, a memory emerged like a whisper from the past. It was a time spent with a cook in a bustling street market, who had often said, "You must know the flavours within you before you can create a dish the world will savour." At that moment, The Seeker recognised that the ingredient missing from their life was a deep and compassionate understanding of themselves, flavours marred by fear and judgment. The Guardian, a wise figure who often guided The Seeker, appeared in their mind's eye, sharing timeless insights about identity and self-perception. "What you see in the mirror is a canvas," The Guardian had said. "Each stroke of self-criticism dulls its colours, while each moment of self-compassion enhances its vibrancy."

This notion of the self as a canvas began to resonate deeply with The Seeker. They realised that the reflections of truth could be both beautiful and harsh, shaped by their own narrative and the narratives imposed by society. As they sat in the park, The Seeker began to explore the shadows in their reflection—the fears of not being enough, of failing in the eyes of others, and of not achieving the dreams they had once held dear. Stripping these fears down to their core revealed a truth: these shadows were not real entities but rather echoes of past experiences and societal pressures. The idea that they were required to conform to certain standards of success or beauty had dictated much of their self-perception. Meanwhile, the light in the reflection—the moments of resilience, creativity, and love—shone brighter than ever. Through moments of vulnerability shared with friends, The Seeker had experienced acceptance and affirmation, which served as catalysts for a transformative understanding of self-worth. "What you embrace in yourself can shatter the illusions imposed by others," The Guardian's voice echoed in their mind. Societal influences on self-image are pervasive, affecting how we perceive our worth and our place in the world. From youth, we are bombarded with messages—through media, social platforms, and even casual conversations—that shape our understanding of what it means to be accepted and validated. These external validations often dictate our inner dialogues.

A glance at social media feeds, filled with curated realities, can lead to toxic comparisons that wreak havoc on our self-esteem. The

We Are Our Own Enemies

Seeker often found themselves ensnared in this web, comparing their unfiltered life with others' highlights, feeling as though they fell short. But awareness, The Guardian reminded, is the first step toward transformation. Recognising the difference between authentic self-perception and the distorted vision fostered by societal standards is crucial. The Seeker slowly began to unearth the layers of conditioned beliefs regarding their identity—unpacking the voice of the critic that had taken residence in their mind. "You are enough," The Guardian would repeat, emphasising the notion that true self-worth is innate, unaffected by external circumstances. As the sun set and the park lights flickered to life, The Seeker gained clarity. They understood that their self-reflection was not merely a solitary battle but the culmination of collective experiences—both personal and societal. In this journey, self-honesty emerged as a guiding principle. Embracing one's flaws alongside strengths is an act of bravery, aligning with a deep-seated understanding of what it means to be human.

Acknowledging both the light and the darkness is essential to self-growth; it allows for a comprehensive view of oneself, enabling the nurturing of inner resilience and compassion. Deepening this dialogue within often requires confronting uncomfortable truths. The decision to look inward, to unravel the threads of negative self-talk, and to recognise triggers for shame and guilt can be daunting. Yet, engaging with these emotions provides valuable insights. The Seeker learned that underneath the fear of inadequacy lay a yearning for authenticity, a desire to be seen and embraced for who they truly were. "Transformative moments arise from moments of discomfort," The Guardian would say with a warm smile. The interplay of light and shadow, not just within oneself but in society—calls for compassion towards both oneself and others. The truth reflected in the mirror also speaks to the unity we share as human beings, illustrating how struggles with self-perception are a universal experience. While The Seeker actively worked on their self-image and perceptions, they couldn't help but recognise that many felt similarly lost in the labyrinth of self-judgment and societal expectations.

A poignant moment arrived during a community event hosted by The Seeker, where individuals shared their own stories of self-doubt and triumph. It was here that they saw the reflections of truth in others—stories filled with vulnerability, heartache, and resilience. Each narrative echoed the same theme: we are often our own worst enemies, yet within these communal exchanges, solace and understanding blossom. As they listened, The Seeker contemplated how each story revealed the shadows that exist in all of us—the fears of inadequacy, the struggle against a harsh internal critic, and the societal pressures that value appearances over authenticity. It was nothing short of enlightening. Each shared struggle created a nourishing space where vulnerability intermingled with strength, highlighting the transformative potential of authentic connection. In embracing these truths—both within themselves and in community—they realised the importance of compassion. To reflect on oneself with honesty is to acknowledge the entirety of the human experience, to embrace flaws while also celebrating victories, however small.

Recognising that shadows are a necessary part of the journey, illuminating the light that must shine through, fosters a deeper understanding of what it means to be whole. How we hold our reflections, then, matters profoundly. Each moment when we choose love over judgment, connection over isolation, we spark a change not only within ourselves but also within our circles. The Seeker learned that the mirror can become a source of empowerment rather than despair, revealing the potential for growth ahead. Ultimately, self-perception is not a static concept; it evolves as we engage with our inner selves honestly and compassionately. It is an invitation to embrace the ongoing exploration of identity, to sit with discomfort, and to celebrate the journey of self-discovery. The Seeker, with guidance from The Guardian and inspired by the stories of others, began to rewrite their narrative—transforming the mirror war into a canvas of self-love and acceptance. With each passing day, they learned to cultivate a practice of self-kindness, bearing witness to their own struggles with grace.

The reflections in the mirror no longer provoked fear but encouraged insight. Recognising the interplay of light and shadow remained essential, reminding them that wholeness encompasses all aspects of being. In this journey, The Seeker also began to share their newfound understanding with others, fostering connections grounded in authenticity and empathy. They discovered that the act of reflecting on oneself isn't solitary; it's a communal endeavour. Together, they could confront societal narratives that undermine true self-worth and cultivate a culture of honesty and compassion. The experiences of The Seeker—navigating through fear, embracing vulnerability, and celebrating resilience—serve as a testament to the power of reflection. This subchapter aims to remind readers that our personal battles are not fought in isolation, but rather resonate through our shared humanity.

The mirror may often hold discomfort, but it can also reveal unprecedented beauty, encouraging us to champion our truths and embrace the fullness of our existence. Navigating the complexities of self-perception, it becomes possible to transform the mirror war into a sanctuary of positivity, fostering a deeper understanding of ourselves and one another. It is here that healing occurs, relationships deepen, and we truly begin to thrive. In the end, honesty and compassion in the face of self-reflection pave the way for us to become our own allies, allowing us to wield the most profound weapon against the enemy within.

The Façade of Identity

In the soft glow of the morning light filtering through the curtains, there lies a duality in every individual: a Protector and a Seeker, each wrestling for dominance in the core of our identity. The Protector, with its sturdy walls and polished surface, stands ready to shield us from the jagged edges of the world, while the Seeker yearns for authenticity, for freedom from the imprisoning façades we so carefully construct. In this dissection of the façades we wear, we delve deep into a realm where self-preservation often leads to self-deception, where the masks we wear to escape vulnerability become our own prisons. Every day, we step out into the world adorned with meticulously crafted identities, woven from societal expectations, past experiences, and a desire for acceptance.

These identities can serve a noble purpose: they protect us from rejection, from humiliation, and from the chilling fear of inadequacy. Yet, unbeknownst to many, these façades can transform into heavy shrouds that obscure our true selves, spurring a profound identity crisis that leaves us feeling lost and disconnected. Let us begin with the Protector, the voice that narrates our defence mechanism against the vulnerability that lies at our core. The Protector insists, "I am here to keep you safe. These masks are not mere costumes; they are shields against a world that can be cruel and unforgiving. You have constructed me out of necessity, and by wearing me, you guard yourself from the pain of exposure. "We recognise the Protector's voice in our own thoughts: "If I show my true self, I might be rejected." The Protector thrives on the fear of visibility, urging us to don a suit of armour that can deflect ridicule and contempt. We readily adopt roles that don't reflect our true selves—whether they manifest as perfectionism in our careers, hyper-competitiveness in social circles, or a stoic demeanour that masks our vulnerability. These roles offer immediate reassurance, falsely promising safety in a precarious landscape. Yet, as we cling tighter to these façades, the lines begin to blur. The Protector tends to overestimate the threat posed by authenticity, convincing us that the temporary solace of being "liked" outweighs the perpetual hunger for self-acceptance. "Isn't it better to be seen for who you are, not than not to be seen at all?" the Protector asks, its voice laden with urgency.

But herein lies the essential paradox: while these façades may shield us from individual scrutiny, they also isolate us from deep connections with others. When living behind a mask, our interactions are tainted by the falsehood of performance. We may become the ideal employee, the picture-perfect parent, or the overachieving student, yet inside, we battle a relentless tide of discontent. This state of being, confined within the prison of our own making, leads to a numbing not just of our vulnerabilities but also of our joys, aspirations, and everyday experiences. The question arises: what happens when the roles we habitually perform become our identity? This is where the Seeker emerges, grappling with the growing dissatisfaction of living inauthentically. "Who am I?" the Seeker cries out during moments of reflection. "Beneath the weight of this façade, I feel like a ghost drifting through life. Is this all there is?" The Seeker's voice carries a profound yearning—one that resonates in quiet moments of introspection when the clamour of external validation fades. It compels us to inquire whether what we present to the world aligns with the essence of our being. This clash of identities can ignite a crisis, where the protective layer we constructed to defend ourselves becomes the very thing that chains us to loneliness and despair.

We Are Our Own Enemies

In times of crises, the Seeker revisits our history—how each traumatic experience, each instance of rejection, has sculpted the façade we wear. "The bullying at school shaped the image of the strong, invulnerable man you show to the world," it whispers, its tone filled with empathy and understanding. "The failure you faced in chasing your dreams taught you to wear the mask of success even when you feel lost. "This reflection unveils another layer to our identities, illustrating how we all wrestle with the jagged pieces of our past that shape our present. The memories strain against the polished surface of the Protector, yearning for recognition, demanding that we face the raw truth of our experiences. What precious insights are we hiding behind our masks? What dreams are buried in the shadows, silenced by the chatter of self-doubt? Yet, as the dialogue between the Protector and the Seeker continues, the Seeker highlights the irony in this struggle: "In shielding myself, I have isolated myself. This mask does not merely hide my vulnerabilities; it also negates my joys." The Seeker understands that while the façade might quell immediate fears and anxieties, it creates an insatiable chasm—a longing for genuine connection that can never be fulfilled as long as we refuse to reveal our authentic selves.

The brave journey of unearthing our true identity can often be terrifying. It requires a willingness to confront our deepest fears, the very things our Protectors guard against—a fear of rejection, of inadequacy, of the unknown. Yet, the Seeker whispers gently, "Real courage lies in vulnerability. Only by exposing ourselves can we forge the bonds we crave." In embracing the raw, untamed aspects of our identities, we can shatter the glass walls we built around ourselves. Yet, peeling off these façades comes with its challenges. The world is not always forgiving; people can harshly judge what they do not understand. The Protector warns us, "What if you expose yourself and find ridicule?" But that very fear can intertwine with our growth. The greatest characters in our stories are often defined not by their successes but by the setbacks and failures they faced on their paths to authenticity. As we draw nearer to the heart of our inquiry, we must confront the consequences of the façades we wear: thunted emotional growth, thaear-laden psyche, and thaervasive feeling of dissonance that manifests in our interactions. We must acknowledge that beneath the protective layers lies a rich tapestry of experience, desire, and authenticity waiting to be unveiled. Imagine stepping into a room filled with voices, laughter, and stories. Your hand trembles as you steady it against the comforting texture of your façade. You can feel the energy in the air, the warmth of connection and understanding, yet the armour weighs heavily on your shoulders.

You yearn to participate, to share your voice, but the Protector growls, "They won't understand. You'll be met with scorn. "But there's a quiet voice within, that of the Seeker, which reminds us that stories connect us deeply. When we allow ourselves to be vulnerable, we invite others to share their authentic selves as well. The façade dissolves, and a new reality emerges—a space where connection flourishes. As we explore further, we encounter the consequences of this disconnect, not just on an individual level, but collectively as a society. Like the fractured pieces of a shattered mirror, our façades complicate human relationships, leading to misunderstandings, divisions, and an escalating sense of loneliness. We have become architects of our own isolation, trapped in a cycle where each mask we don serves to separate us from one another. Herein lies the pivotal question: how long can we persist in living behind these façades without losing sight of our true selves? This constant masquerade can eventually overshadow our lives, leading to identity crises that challenge our perceptions of self-worth, purpose, and a sense of belonging. What we need, then, is a bridge—a passage between our identities.

This is where the journey to authenticity paves the way for healing —a slow and deliberate process of unmasking that requires patience, courage, and, above all else, self-compassion. How can we begin to honour our vulnerabilities while still embracing the strong parts of ourselves? The answer lies in turning the volume down on the Protector's voice while amplifying the Seeker's gentle inquiries. It calls us to explore the edges of our façades, testing the waters of authenticity, and discovering that in moments of vulnerability, we can really just be ourselves. The world outside may not always react as we hope, yet within those moments of authenticity lies the seed of connection, of shared experience and mutual understanding. Let's revisit that room filled with laughter and stories. Imagine stepping in, shedding your protective layers—from the false narratives of success to the constant comparisons that breed envy and insecurity. What if you allowed yourself to be visible, to speak your truth? Quieting the Protector can feel like an act of rebellion, a leap into uncertainty. But what awaits is far greater—an invitation into a shared journey of authenticity, where the walls of division crumble, and we connect over our shared struggles and triumphs. As we begin to embrace the uncomfortable pangs of vulnerability, we can cultivate a newfound sense of identity that is not predicated on worldly validation but rather grounded in internal worthiness. Through this exploration, we witness a transformation—a gradual acceptance of the beautiful complexities that make us human. No longer confined to a single narrative, our identities become a rich mosaic of experiences, emotions, and aspirations. But this journey is not without hesitation; moments of uncertainty will arise as we confront what we've long concealed.

We Are Our Own Enemies

The Protector will, undoubtedly, voice its concern: "You are exposing yourself to pain!" And yet, the Seeker gently pushes back, reminding us that the healing begins at the edges of vulnerability. It's in exposing the scars and the imperfections that we find a community of shared experiences. It is here that we discover a new kind of strength—one that doesn't hide or embellish but embraces and rebuilds. As we move forward, the process of unmasking means being willing to challenge our long-held beliefs—beliefs about who we must be to be loved or accepted. These beliefs shape not just our individual realities but also the collective narrative we share. It calls into question how we engage in the world, the way we connect with others, and the legacy we leave behind. We must stand firm as we merge the voices of the Protector and the Seeker, allowing them to coexist rather than reign in opposition. Together, they can foster an understanding that embracing authenticity does not mean discarding the tools that once protected us; instead, it means learning to wield them responsibly. The Protector can transform into a guardian of authenticity, finding strength in the vulnerability that the Seeker discovers.

In fostering this integration, the journey towards authenticity becomes a communal one. As we share our truths, we invite others to do the same, creating a ripple effect—a movement towards deeper understanding and compassion fuelled by our collective stories. In closing, we return to the concept of identity and the masks we wear. The Protector may always linger in the background, but it is the Seeker's gentle ambition for authenticity that holds the promise of liberation. As we peel back the layers of façade, we not only discover ourselves anew but also forge stronger connections with others—a beautiful testament to the strength found in shared vulnerability. We may find, at the journey's end, that what we initially guarded so fiercely—the tender parts of our existence—

become the very threads that weave us together and enrich our shared humanity. And through this unmasking, we transform not just as individuals but as a collective, moving away from the farce of isolated identities towards embracing the wholeness of human experience. It is here, in the delicate interplay between our identities, that we become more than our fears—we become a symphony of authenticity, weaving our unique stories into a harmonious narrative.

The Path to Acceptance

The journey toward self-acceptance is one of the most profound paths one can take. It is a road often fraught with obstacles, self-doubt, and the lingering echoes of past hurts. However, it is also a path lined with opportunities for growth, healing, and transformation. As we navigate this journey, it is essential to recognise that self-acceptance is not merely about embracing our positive attributes but also about reconciling our flaws, mistakes, and insecurities with our true essence. One of the first steps on this path is acknowledging our self-image. Often, we find ourselves trapped in a distorted reflection, much like the distortion of a funhouse mirror. We may focus on our perceived inadequacies while disregarding the beauty and strength that reside within us. To mend this fracture between self-image and true essence, we must cultivate a sense of self-awareness that allows us to see ourselves with clarity.

Practising mindfulness can be an invaluable tool in this process. Mindfulness encourages us to observe our thoughts and feelings without judgment, allowing us to uncover the truth about our self-image. This can involve simple exercises such as sitting in a quiet space and focusing on our breath. With each inhale, we invite a sense of acceptance, and with each exhale, we release self-criticism and negativity. As we become more attuned to our internal dialogues, we can begin to identify the harmful thoughts that contribute to a distorted self-image. One practical exercise is to keep a self-reflection journal. Allocate a few minutes each day to write down your thoughts and feelings about yourself. Begin by noting down the positive aspects you appreciate about yourself. Be specific, focusing on qualities that may seem small but are meaningful to you. This could include your ability to listen, your creativity, or your sense of humour. Once you have listed these strengths, move on to reflect on the areas you struggle with. Write about your insecurities or perceived failures. Rather than judging or criticising yourself during this process, approach it with compassion.

This dual perspective allows you to engage in a dialogue with yourself—a key component in reconciling self-image with true essence. As we venture deeper into the path of self-acceptance, we may uncover wounds from the past that contribute to our skewed self-perception. Previous experiences of criticism, failure, or rejection can linger long after they occur, shaping our current self-perception. The Guardian, a metaphorical figure representing wisdom and awareness, can guide us in navigating these past hurts. The Guardian encourages us to face our pain, not by avoiding it, but by examining it with curiosity and tenderness. One approach to confronting past hurts is through the practice of forgiveness. Forgiveness is often misunderstood; it does not mean condoning the pain inflicted upon us, but rather releasing the hold that these experiences have on our lives. This begins with forgiving ourselves for any perceived failures or shortcomings. Write a letter to yourself expressing understanding and compassion for your past decisions and mistakes.

We Are Our Own Enemies

Allow yourself the grace to be human and recognise that growth often comes through struggle. In addition to self-forgiveness, it is equally important to forgive others who have hurt us. This may involve writing a letter to the person who caused us pain, even if we never intend to send it. The act of expressing our feelings—acknowledging the hurt, anger, or disappointment—serves to unburden our hearts. This release can help dissolve the bitterness that clouds our self-perception. Yet, even as we embrace this forgiveness, it is crucial to address our flaws directly. Embracing our imperfections is a pivotal part of the journey to self-acceptance. Oftentimes, we are conditioned to believe that we must be perfect or conform to societal ideals. However, our flaws—our vulnerabilities—are what make us human and relatable. The Guardian invites us to celebrate these imperfections, viewing them as unique aspects of our character rather than shortcomings. An exercise to aid this acceptance of flaws involves creating a "Flaws and Strengths" inventory.

On one side of a piece of paper, write down the qualities you perceive as flaws. On the opposite side, list the strengths that counterbalance these perceived weaknesses. For instance, if you consider yourself to be overly sensitive, recognise that this sensitivity also translates to deep empathy and the ability to connect with others on a profound level. This exercise reinforces the idea that we are complex beings with both strengths and weaknesses coexisting in harmony. Cultivating self-love is another essential aspect of the path to acceptance. Self-love is not about vanity or arrogance; it is the practice of treating ourselves with the same kindness and respect that we would offer a friend. The Guardian reminds us that self-love is foundational to mental resilience, as it fosters a belief in our worthiness, regardless of external circumstances. A practical strategy to nurture self-love is to develop affirmations that resonate deeply with you. Create a list of positive statements that reflect your inherent worth and value. Examples might include: "I am enough," "I deserve love and kindness," or "I am worthy of my dreams."

Recite these affirmations daily, particularly during moments of self-doubt or criticism. Over time, these positive assertions can rewire our internal dialogue, gradually replacing self-deprecating thoughts with encouragement and support. Furthermore, self-care plays a pivotal role in fostering self-love. Engage in activities that nourish your body, mind, and spirit. This could involve regular exercise, which releases endorphins and boosts self-esteem, or indulging in hobbies that bring you joy. Establish boundaries that protect your well-being, ensuring that you prioritise your needs and desires. As our journey unfolds, it is important to surround ourselves with positive influences. Being mindful of the relationships we cultivate can greatly impact our path to acceptance. Seek out connections that uplift you and encourage self-discovery. These individuals should celebrate your uniqueness and support your growth. Conversely, distance yourself from relationships that foster negativity, judgment, or comparison. The Guardian symbolises the wisdom within us to discern which relationships contribute to our journey and which detract from it. Incorporating creativity into our self-acceptance journey can also have a profound effect. Artistic expression—whether through painting, writing, dancing, or any other form—allows us to explore and express our inner selves. It can serve as both an outlet for emotions and a way to uncover deeper truths about our identity.

Consider engaging in creative projects that reflect your experiences, dreams, and aspirations. This creative exploration can provide insight into how you perceive yourself and can foster a sense of acceptance. As we embrace our flaws and nurture self-love, it is essential to cultivate resilience. Hardships and setbacks inevitably punctuate life, and our self-perception largely influences our ability to bounce back from adversity. When we view ourselves with compassion and acceptance, we equip ourselves with the mental and emotional tools needed to face life's challenges head-on. To build resilience, consider practising gratitude. Focusing on what we are thankful for shifts our perspective and fosters a sense of abundance rather than one of scarcity or lack. Start a gratitude journal where you note down three things you are grateful for each day. This can be particularly powerful on difficult days when self-doubt may creep in. By consciously recognising the positives, we reinforce a belief in our worth and capacity to overcome challenges. Visualisation is another powerful tool in nurturing resilience and fostering self-acceptance.

Create a mental image of your ideal self—one who embodies confidence, compassion, and self-love. Spend time visualising this version of yourself navigating the world with grace and strength. This practice not only allows you to cultivate a clearer image of who you strive to be but also empowers you to take actionable steps toward that vision. As we conclude our exploration of "The Path to Acceptance," remember that this journey is deeply personal and unique to each individual. It is a path marked by self-discovery, healing, and growth, with the Guardian within guiding us at every step. Embrace the understanding that self-acceptance is an ongoing process, one that requires patience, compassion, and commitment. The road may be long, and the winds of self-criticism may occasionally threaten to blow us off course, but with each step we take toward acceptance, we pave the way for a healthier self-perception and stronger mental resilience. In confronting and embracing our flaws, engaging in practices of self-love, and nurturing our resilience, we honour the truth of who we are—complex, imperfect, and beautifully human.

As you embark on this journey, invite yourself to be a gentle companion to your own heart. Offer grace in moments of struggle and rejoice in the small victories along the way. Each step forward is a testament to your courage, and with time, you will find that self-acceptance is not just a destination, but a lifelong journey of discovery, healing, and love.

Fear: The Silent Killer of Dreams

The Roots of Fear

Fear is an innate human emotion, one that has been hardwired into our biology since the dawn of our species. It is a primal instinct that serves to protect us from danger, but its roots extend far deeper, intertwining with our experiences, societal expectations, and the intricate tales of our lives. In tracing the origins of fear, we uncover a tapestry woven from childhood moments, parental expectations, cultural narratives, and the often-unforgiving standards imposed by society. This exploration reveals not only where our fears originate but also how these fears shape our ambitions and decisions as we mature into adulthood.

Many of our childhood memories are infused with vivid emotions that can linger long into our adult years. For instance, consider the day when a young child takes their first steps. The bright smiles and encouraging cheers from family and friends often overshadow the moments of hesitance and timidity. However, the early significant milestones of our lives also bear the shadow of doubt—what if I fall? What if no one is there to catch me? In these formative years, fear begins to rear its head. Rather than developing courage, a child may internalise the belief that risk leads to pain or failure, and thus begins the pattern of avoiding fear-inducing situations.

Parental figures often play a crucial role in shaping our responses to fear. A well-meaning parent may aim to protect their child from harm, warning them against various dangers, both real and perceived. While these warnings can prevent physical dangers, they can also teach children to approach the world with trepidation. A simple phrase like "Don't talk to strangers" can morph into generalised anxiety, instilling a fear of the unknown that persists long after childhood ends. The child grows into adulthood with a wariness of new experiences, fearing not just potential dangers but the discomfort of unfamiliarity. Those who grow up under the weight of overprotective parenting often find themselves wrestling with a profound fear of failure, believing that attempting something new may lead to disappointment and shame.

As we continue through life, the fears ingrained in us from childhood do not dissolve in the face of increasing maturity; rather, they evolve and adapt in response to societal pressures. Conforming to societal expectations can generate a landscape rife with anxiety. The quest for approval and acceptance, particularly during adolescence, stirs an underlying fear of being judged unworthy or inadequate. A teenager who aspires to excel academically may find themselves paralysed by the fear of not meeting the lofty standards set by parents, teachers, or even peers. Instead of viewing education as a pathway to growth, they might regard it as a high-stakes performance—one that determines their worth.

From academic achievement to personal relationships, societal expectations are rarely kind to those who dare to defy the norm. The culture of comparison in today's social media-driven world amplifies this phenomenon. As individuals scroll through perfectly curated lives displayed online, the fear of not measuring up is thrust into sharp relief, leading to crippling self-doubt. The result is an inner dialogue that often echoes the voices of those who imposed their expectations on us during childhood. The previously learned patterns of avoidance take on new forms; we can become averse to pursuing our dreams for fear of ridicule or failure, which ultimately leads us to stay in our comfort zones, stifling ambition and growth.

We Are Our Own Enemies

The psychological perspectives on fear provide valuable insights into its origins and manifestations. The American Psychological Association defines fear as an emotional response to an immediate threat, while anxiety operates as a response to potential threats or perceived dangers. This subtle but pivotal distinction emphasises that fear can manifest not only in direct encounters with danger but also through the anticipation of what might come. Fear as an anticipatory response can lead to various debilitating conditions, including phobias, social anxiety, and obsessive-compulsive behaviours. Research has identified that early traumatic experiences can predispose individuals to heightened fear responses later in life. For example, children who witness domestic violence may grow into adults with an exaggerated startle response; they develop a hyper-vigilant approach to their surroundings, always anticipating danger. These learned responses can lead to self-sabotaging behaviours, as the individual often seeks to avoid situations that may trigger memories of their trauma, thus hampering their ambitions and pursuit of happiness.

Moreover, the concept of the "fearful avoidant attachment style," developed by psychologists John Bowlby and Mary Ainsworth, provides further clarity on how fear influences our relationships. Individuals with this attachment style often struggle with intimacy and trust due to fear of rejection or abandonment. The roots of such behaviour are often traced back to inconsistent caregiving during formative years, where love was meted out conditionally. As these individuals mature, they may subconsciously replicate the cycle, sabotaging intimate connections out of fear of vulnerability and the potential for subsequent heartache.

Navigating through life's challenges, we often find that these fears manifest in subtle yet profound ways. In my own journey, I vividly recall an instance from my early career that encapsulates the complexities of fear intertwined with anticipation and societal expectations. When I first dared to share my writing with others—my deepest thoughts and insecurities framed in prose—I was overwhelmed by a torrent of fear. The anticipation of facing critique felt like standing on the edge of a precipice, each heartbeat echoing the worry, "What if my words fail to resonate? What if they're ridiculed?" This reluctance stemmed not only from my self-doubt but also from the flurry of societal expectations. Would my work measure up to established authors? Would it find a place among the voices that already crowded the literary landscape?

Such moments are a testament to how fear acts as both servant and master. It can become a servant when it motivates us to prepare and improve—practicing our craft, researching diligently, or honing our skills. Yet, it can easily morph into a master, imprisoning us within our own insecurities. I chose to submit my work, but the journey to that decision felt like traversing a minefield—anxiety and anticipation working against each other. The outcome, while ultimately rewarding, was shaped by my willingness to confront the very fears that sought to undermine my endeavour.

Fear can also distort our perception of success. The societal constructs of what success looks like often exacerbate fear. If our vision of success is tightly woven with external validation—like income levels, job titles, or societal accolades—we risk equating our self-worth with our accomplishments. The fear of failure, thus, can immobilise us, leading to patterns of procrastination. We may convince ourselves that we cannot attempt something unless we are sure we will succeed, but this mindset only perpetuates a cycle of stagnation. The irony is that in preventing risks associated with potential failure, we may also forfeit opportunities for growth and the possibility of achieving our true desires.

We Are Our Own Enemies

Understanding the multifaceted nature of fear can be a radical game-changer in how we approach our lives. It invites us to examine the roots of our fears with a discerning eye, dismantling the narratives we've held onto throughout the years. It encourages us to recognise that fear, while a part of the human experience, does not have to dictate our choices or our futures.

One effective strategy to address our fears involves reframing. By shifting our perspective on fear—it does not signify weakness but rather a reflection of our aspirations—we can approach life's challenges with renewed vitality. For example, instead of succumbing to the fear of public speaking, consider it an opportunity for connection. Lean into the discomfort and explore the rich terrain beyond fear's confines. Learning to identify what excites us beyond the initial anxiety can help us view situations not as threats, but as potential avenues for growth and development.

At its core, embracing fear involves a continuous dance between recognition and action. It may mean sitting with the discomfort of anxiety while also committing to taking small, intentional steps towards our goals. Instead of allowing fear to anchor us, we can use it as a springboard—a source of energy that propels us forward. Empathy can serve as an illuminating force in our journey to understand fear within ourselves and others. When we witness the fears of those around us, we foster an environment of vulnerability and openness, which can be radically healing. Whether through sharing our own stories or encouraging others to voice their fears, we can begin to reclaim power over those fears that seek to limit us. The act of opening up can dissolve the perceived isolation that fear often breeds. The exploration of fear invites us to rewrite our narratives. It encourages agility in thinking, fostering resilience and empathy. In doing so, we learn to view our fears not as insurmountable barriers but as human experiences we can transcend together. The shadows cast by fear begin to recede as we confront our personal and societal barriers head-on. The journey of understanding fear becomes less about overcoming it entirely and more about coexisting with it, proving that our ambitions and dreams are still within reach, despite its haunting presence.

In the end, as we peel back the layers of fear and delve into its origins, we unveil a path towards healing—a path not solely for ourselves but for those who walk beside us. It is in this shared experience that we cultivate compassion, learning to champion both our journeys and those of others, transforming fear from a silent killer of dreams into an ally in the pursuit of the life we desire. Embracing this new narrative offers us a clearer lens through which to view the world: one where fear, rather than a foe, can eventually become a treasured companion on our journey to thriving.

Confronting the Shadows

Fear often lurks in the shadows, quietly stealing our dreams and paralysing our potential. It thrives in the dark corners of our minds, often masquerading as rational thought or caution. To accomplish anything meaningful, we must confront these shadows directly, rather than allowing them to dictate the course of our lives. In this subchapter, we will explore various strategies to face our fears head-on, challenge their validity, and ultimately transform them into sources of empowerment.

The first step in confronting fear is identification. Fear can sometimes be vague, a heavy feeling in your stomach that lacks a tangible source. To combat this intangible foe, start by taking a moment to reflect on what specifically instills that feeling in you. Is it a fear of failure, rejection, loneliness, or perhaps the unknown? By naming your fear, you begin to weaken its power over you. Write it down; articulate it in a few simple words. The act of naming it creates a boundary, allowing you to both acknowledge it and distance yourself from its paralysing effects.

Once you have identified your fear, it's crucial to challenge its validity. Fears can often be exaggerated or rooted in past experiences that no longer have relevance to your current situation. Ask yourself a few important questions: What evidence do I have that this fear is rational? How likely is it that the worst-case scenario actually occurs? What is the worst that could happen, and how would I cope with that situation? By dissecting your fear logically, you can often see that the outcomes you dread are far less likely than your mind may convince you. Consider the power of reframing your perspective. Instead of looking at fear as a barrier, view it as a signal that you are on the brink of growth. Every time you feel fear, recognise it as an opportunity to stretch beyond your comfort zone. For instance, if public speaking terrifies you, think of it as a chance to connect with others and share your valuable insights. This shift in mindset alone can be transformative, turning fear—an emotion that could hinder progress—into a catalyst for action.

After identifying and reframing your fear, it's time to take action, but remember to start small. Instead of trying to conquer your fear in one fell swoop, break it down into manageable steps. If your goal is to become more social but you fear meeting new people, begin with small but courageous actions. Attend a gathering with a friend, engage in small talk with a stranger, or practice introducing yourself. Each small step is akin to shining a flashlight into the dark corners where fear hides. The more light you shed through action, the smaller and less intimidating those shadows become.

The power of small victories cannot be overstated. Each seemingly minor accomplishment helps build your confidence and diminishes the hold fear has over you. Create a list of achievable steps that lead towards your goal, and check them off as you complete them. Celebrate these victories, no matter how small they may seem. They are the fundamental building blocks of transformation.

In this journey of confronting our fears, personal stories can serve as powerful sources of inspiration. Take, for instance, the story of Linda, a woman paralysed by a fear of failure that prevented her from pursuing her dream career in art. For years, she allowed her fears to dictate her life choices, working in a job that offered security but no fulfilment. One day, after attending a workshop on creativity and vulnerability, Linda decided enough was enough. She began to explore her fears through journaling. In her writings, she articulated the deepest insecurities that drove her decision-making. Was she terrified of failing as an artist, or was she more afraid of regretting never trying at all? Armed with this new perspective, she took action. Linda committed to creating one piece of artwork each week, no matter how imperfect it was. She began sharing her work with friends and family, first privately, then on social media. With each piece, Linda grew more confident and found a supportive community that celebrated her creativity.

Eventually, she participated in an art exhibition. The day of the event was filled with anxiety, but instead of succumbing to her fears, Linda confronted them with courage. She was nervous but excited. The moment she entered the gallery and saw her artwork displayed on the walls, she felt a rush of empowerment that surpassed all her fears. Hundreds of eyes were admiring her work, acknowledging her journey, and for the first time, she understood that her fear of failure was minuscule in comparison to the fulfillment she felt in embracing her passion.

We Are Our Own Enemies

Linda's story serves as a testament to the life-changing power of confronting fear. By articulating her fears, reframing them, and taking small steps, she overcame what once held her captive. We can also draw inspiration from the journey of Dr Neil Sutton, a renowned psychologist who spent much of his career studying the impact of fear on behaviour. In his seminars, he often shares a deeply personal anecdote about his own fear of public speaking—ironically, a fear he encountered frequently in his vocation. Despite his expertise, he struggled with anxiety every time he stepped onto a stage. To combat this fear, Dr Sutton developed a simple yet effective strategy. He set a goal to speak publicly at least once every month. He approached each opportunity as a learning experience rather than a performance that required perfection. He began inviting honest feedback from attendees, focusing not on criticism but on constructive conversation. As he routinely faced this fear, the once overwhelming anxiety transformed into excitement. Today, Dr Sutton speaks confidently on international platforms, inspiring others to confront their fears and to embrace vulnerability.

Confronting fear isn't just about personal narratives; it's also essential to understand the broader impact fear has on our lives and how its root causes often intertwine. As people, we are shaped by cultural narratives that instill fears regarding failure, rejection, and even success. The compelling allure of societal approval can often resonate silently in our decision-making processes, breeding anxiety about living authentically. Recognising these external influences enables us to address and overcome them, regaining control.

To further assist in facing fear, visualisation techniques can prove exceptionally powerful. Take time each day to sit in a quiet space, close your eyes, and visualise yourself overcoming a specific fear. Picture it in vivid detail: the surroundings, the emotions you experience, and especially the triumphant outcome. Imagine each step involved in facing this fear and visualise yourself succeeding. This practice not only prepares your mind for real-life situations but also helps reinforce a positive outcome in your subconscious—a vital element in reprogramming your response to fear.

Another potent tool for confronting fear is mindfulness. Engaging in mindfulness practices—such as meditation, deep breathing, or yoga—creates the mental space necessary for introspection. These practices help ground you in the present moment, allowing you to observe your fears without judgment. When you practice mindfulness, you become more adept at managing your emotions, enabling you to respond to fear with clarity rather than reaction. This state of self-awareness opens the door to understanding your fears and equips you with the resilience to face them more effectively.

Support networks can also play a pivotal role in confronting fear. Surround yourself with individuals who uplift and encourage you. When you share your fears with others—be it friends, family, or even support groups—you realise that you are not alone in your struggles. Vulnerability breeds connection, and by voicing your fears, you often gain new perspectives that lighten the emotional load you carry. When others share their experiences with fear, it can be immensely encouraging, allowing you to relate and seek strength from collective struggles.

As you embark on this journey of confronting the shadows of fear, consider the concept of "fear-setting," a technique popularised by author and entrepreneur Tim Ferris. Fear-setting involves not only identifying the fear you wish to confront but also outlining the worst-case scenario, the likelihood of its occurrence, and how you would address it if it were to happen. This technique helps create a balanced risk assessment, enabling you to weigh the potential risks against the cost of inaction. It's a method for reframing fear to motivate rather than deter you.

In conclusion, confronting fear is not an easy task, but it requires dedication, introspection, and a willingness to step outside comfort zones. As you begin to acknowledge your fears, challenge their foundation, embrace small victories, and learn from personal stories, you will undoubtedly find the courage necessary to face what once felt insurmountable. Fear, when met with action and understanding, can shift from being a barrier to being a guiding force for personal and communal growth. So, take a deep breath, acknowledge the shadows lurking within, and step boldly into the light of courage and empowerment. In doing so, you don't just confront what frightens you; you pave the way for a more fulfilling and authentic life. Together, we can turn fear into a catalyst for transformation, becoming our own allies in the pursuit of dreams and possibilities.

The Cost of Inaction

In the quiet corners of our minds, fear often whispers insidiously, weaving narratives that hinder our progress and keep our dreams at bay. While fear serves a protective purpose, shielding us from potential harm, it can also morph into a paralysing force that stifles our aspirations. The voices of doubt and insecurity grow louder, drowning out the chorus of hope and possibility. This internal struggle leads to a profound question: What is the true cost of inaction?

When we examine our lives, it is not the moments of failure that we regret most, but rather the opportunities we let slip through our fingers because we chose not to act. The tales of those who have experienced this dolorous reality serve as cautionary reminders—a tapestry of dreams deferred and lives lived in inaction. Consider the story of a young woman named Maya, who harboured dreams of pursuing a career in the arts. As a child, her creativity flowed unabashedly. She painted, danced, and wrote, unrestricted by the constraints of the adult world. Yet, as she transitioned into her teenage years, the growing spectre of fear began to suffocate her spirit.

Maya's protective voice, draped in the guise of practicality, cautioned her against pursuing the arts. "You need a stable job," it whispered. "What if you fail? You won't survive in such an unstable industry." These messages, echoed by well-meaning family and societal expectations, gradually drowned out her own desires. The more she listened, the less she believed in the possibility of her dreams. She chose to study business instead, prioritising security over passion.

Years passed, and Maya found herself in a corporate job that was comfortable yet soul-draining. Each day was a muted reflection of her vibrant self. On weekends, she would attend art workshops and community theatres, feeling her passion ignited only to be extinguished by the looming thoughts of Monday morning. Each time a friend suggested a project, her fear spoke louder than her dreams. "What if no one likes your work?" it echoed. "What if it's not good enough?" And, time and again, she opted for inaction.

Maya's story is woven with regret; she watched as the creative fire she once had flickered dimly. Her most painful realisation came during a quiet night when she found herself staring at blank canvases, yearning to unleash the stories in her heart. What she noticed most was the absence of her own voice—the once daring dreamer replaced by a puppet of fear. She understood in that moment that her decision to remain in her comfort zone exacted a heavy toll: her spirit, like a bird caged by its own fears, was trapped.

We Are Our Own Enemies

As we navigate through our lives, Maya's experience resonates with many of us, revealing a universal truth: inaction born from fear leads to a profound sense of loss. The regret of a dream not pursued, of passions unfulfilled, echoes loudly in the chambers of our hearts. But it does not stop there. The ramifications of inaction extend beyond our personal feelings; they ripple outward, affecting our relationships, our communities, and even our world.

When we allow fear to dictate our actions, we unintentionally foster disconnection and stagnation. We become spectators in our own lives, side-lining not just our dreams but also our ability to contribute meaningfully to the lives around us. Take, for instance, the story of a community leader named Thomas, who was once brimming with ideas for local initiatives aimed at fostering unity among diverse groups. Although he envisioned a vibrant neighbourhood where cultures intertwined, fear silenced his voice.

What if no one showed up to his meetings? What if people resisted change? These thoughts knotted in his stomach, and instead of organising a community event to promote understanding through dialogue, he stayed silent. Days turned into months, and the divide in his neighbourhood grew wider, with fear and misunderstanding breeding hostility. Thomas eventually watched as his once-thriving community succumbed to isolation and division. Each moment of inaction built a wall between neighbours. He came to realise that by allowing fear to hold him captive, he inadvertently contributed to the very separation he longed to mend.

The narrative of inaction is woven with threads of collective broader implications. When individuals like Thomas hesitate, the cumulative effect can be staggering. A failure to act on ideas, advocacy, or innovation chips away at the potential for growth and development within communities. It is an egregious irony: in prioritising safety and security, we often end up fostering stagnation and division, amplifying a different kind of danger—a lack of progress.

The fear-driven inaction we engage in not only stifles our personal growth but also curtails the collective progress of humanity. When we examine the historical tapestry of social change, it becomes apparent that change makers faced fears of rejection, failure, and ridicule. From civil rights activists to innovators in the business world, it is clear that those who took risks and acted despite fear helped shape the world we live in today. Their courage stands in stark contrast to the consequences of inaction—a journey marked by frustrating stagnation and unfulfilled potential.

As we deliberate on our fears, we must ask ourselves: Is it truly safer to stay where we are, or does inaction come with its own set of hazards? It's crucial to evaluate the costs of remaining static in our lives, weighed against the uncertainties of pursuing our dreams. Fear can only have power over us if we let it—a lesson Maya eventually learned. After years of nurturing regret, she sought help to confront her fears and rekindle her passions. This path was not devoid of uncertainty. But with each brushstroke on the canvas, she began to reclaim her voice amid the chaotic noise of apprehension.

The shift in perspective allowed her to weigh the costs of inaction against the potential benefits of taking risks. As she painted fearlessly, she remembered how invigorating the act of creation felt. Every completed piece of art became a testament to confronting fear and embracing possibility. She realised that a life lived in pursuit of passion, despite fear's incessant whispers, held the potential for fulfilment beyond her wildest dreams.

Encouragement flourished in the spaces where fear was met with action. Maya's renewed enthusiasm led her to host her own art show, where vulnerable narratives unfolded through her paintings. The community that once felt distant drew nearer as individuals connected over shared stories and experiences. Together, they battled the fear of being misunderstood and found courage in creativity. By choosing to act despite fear, Maya not only reclaimed her dreams but also fostered a sense of connection that reverberated through the hearts of those around her.

This narrative underscores a profound truth—action is a catalyst for transformation. When we acknowledge our fears but decide to move forward anyway, we open new pathways of opportunity and connection. In contemplating the cost of inaction, we must shift our focus from the risks we perceive to the opportunities that arise from taking bold steps. As we explore this dynamic, it becomes clear that fears, while formidable, often pale in comparison to the benefits of taking risks for our dreams.

Finding the courage to act requires conscious choices—embracing discomfort, acknowledging fear, and still stepping out of our comfort zones. It also necessitates a deliberate effort to envision the life we want to create. What if we dared to imagine what our world could look like if we chose action over inaction? By visualising our desired outcomes, we weaken the hold of fear. In doing so, we can clearly see the vibrant tapestry of possibilities expanding before us.

We must approach fear not as an enemy to be vanquished but as a companion on our journey—a flawed yet necessary aspect of being human. In this light, fear can serve as a compass. It signals the edge of our comfort zones and illuminates areas where growth and expansion await. When we confront our fears and navigate them with informed action, we empower ourselves and reclaim ownership of our dreams.

We Are Our Own Enemies

The culmination of these efforts may lead us to a powerful realisation: inaction does not keep us safe; rather, it confines us, restricting our ability to live truly. The vibrant life of our dreams awaits on the other side of fear. To fully invest in our lives and communities, we must consciously choose to act despite uncertainties. In the act of striving, we create not only a life worth living but also open the door for others to do the same.

Consider the costs of inaction as a severe price paid for silence. The dreams we harbour are not solely ours; they are seeds of potential meant to blossom for ourselves and others. As we reclaim agency over our lives and visions, we can spark a chain reaction of inspiration within our communities, awakening the dormant dreams of others and igniting collective empowerment.

In closing, we return to the stories—the countless individuals who have succeeded against the odds by daring to act despite their fears. While fear may always exist as a backdrop, it is action that brings colour to our narratives. Like Maya, who transformed hesitation into artistry, or Thomas, who stepped forward to unite his community, we can choose courage over comfort. The cost of inaction may seem attractive in its promise of safety, but the vibrant landscapes of possibility that await on the other side—a world rich in passion and connection—far outweigh the fears that seek to hold us back.

It is time to embrace action with open hearts, to silence the voices of fear with the resounding drum of our dreams. Each step forward is a declaration: "I choose to live. I choose to pursue my passion. I choose to inspire." Let this be a call to make our lives a testament to the beauty of taking risks, living boldly, and sowing dreams into the fabric of our realities. In the end, the dream denied is the inevitable regret; the dream pursued transforms into the vibrant reality we can share with the world.

The Prison of Doubt

Unravelling Self-Doubt

The Seeker sat alone in a quiet café, a small haven amidst the bustling world outside. The aroma of freshly brewed coffee mixed with the scent of baked pastries, yet none of it reached The Seeker's senses. Instead, a storm brewed within. In the soft glow of the overhead lights, shadowy figures danced on the surface of thoughts, each one a manifestation of doubt, whispering insidious tales of inadequacy and failure. "Who do you think you are?" one voice sneered, its tone laced with venom. "You'll never amount to anything." The Seeker pushed these thoughts down, gritting teeth and tightening fists, but the shadows persisted, swirling into a tempest that threatened to engulf all dreams.

In the far corner of the café, a young mother juggled her toddler while reading a book, and The Seeker could not help but compare their lives. The effortless ease with which she smiled, the way she engaged with her child, filled The Seeker with an overwhelming sense of inadequacy. "Why can't you be more like her?" the voices taunted, each jab etching deeper lines of self-doubt across an already weary heart.

The café echoed with laughter and conversations, yet The Seeker felt alien, ensnared in an invisible cage crafted from the very thoughts that were supposed to propel one forward. It was here, in this enforced solitude, that an understanding began to dawn: self-doubt had become an uninvited guest, whispering vicious lies and distorting reality.

Self-doubt is a powerful force, an enemy that often materialises in seemingly innocuous moments, simmering beneath the surface of daily life. The Seeker had spent years learning to navigate this enemy, yet the struggle was always there—one flicker of insecurity igniting a wildfire of hesitance. Dreams began to blur; aspirations lost their vibrancy under the weight of an internal critique that rarely dulled. Through the lens of personal experiences, it became apparent that self-doubt can cripple potential in insidious ways. The Seeker began reflecting on moments when opportunities arose, only to recede into the safety of what was known, paralysed by a fear of judgment and failure. The job interview that was so close, yet never pursued; the relationship that fled because vulnerability felt too raw; the dream to write a novel that was shelved indefinitely, buried under layers of "What if?"

As The Seeker contemplated these moments, storytelling emerged as a necessary tool to unravel the curtain of self-doubt. Words unfurled into a vivid landscape, allowing The Seeker to paint the essence of insecurity as a tangible enemy. Once, The Seeker stood at the edge of a vast stage, a sea of faces looming from the darkness beyond the spotlight. Every eye felt like a piercing gaze, and every whisper seemed to dissect personal stories into shards. Nerves quaked in the pit of the stomach, amplifying an acute awareness that stunted creativity and expression. Doubt materialised, becoming a creature lurking in the shadows, ready to trip over each word, leading The Seeker to an inevitable downfall. "It's only in your head," friends had said. "Just relax, you'll be fine." Yet those words barely scratched the surface of a festering wound. The Seeker had internalised the belief that any vulnerability would expose weakness, allowing doubt to run rampant, shrouding potential like a thick fog.

Through the lens of psychology, various theories on self-doubt emerged, unravelling the complex nature of this insidious enemy. Albert Bandura's concept of self-efficacy provided a foundation: one's belief in capability could either elevate aspirations or sink

We Are Our Own Enemies

ambitions into the mire of defeat. When faced with challenges, The Seeker realised that doubt stripped away confidence, resulting in a self-fulfilling prophecy where negative expectations overshadowed opportunities. The Seeker had become acutely aware of the feedback loop created by self-doubt. Each moment of hesitation bred further uncertainty. In achieving small victories, however, an unanticipated shift began to emerge. The Seeker would return to the foundations of self-efficacy, challenging each detracting thought with evidence, and slowly, the whispers began to drown out in the realisation of capability. Echoes of the past surfaced; each time The Seeker had confronted fear, each battle fought against the oppressive silence inside led to victories, albeit small. With every pencil stroke on a blank page or every footfall onto a stage, the narrative of self-doubt shifted from an ominous presence to a minor plot point. The realisation that these shadows could not be eliminated but transformed into allies became a guiding light toward growth. The metaphorical landscape continued to shift; doubt morphed from a monstrous figure into a malleable entity that could be conversed with, understood, and ultimately diminished. Each reflection and inner dialogue fed the resolve to challenge the fears head-on. The Seeker embarked on a quest to dissect every shade of self-doubt. It was essential to dissect the roots. In one particular moment, an old journal resurfaced from the abandoned recesses of a past self. The pages were a tapestry woven from insecurities, heartbreaks, and dreams that had fallen to dust, but they illuminated a clear pathway - the journey through self-doubt was not a solitary one. Everyone shared the common thread of grappling with uncertainty.

As The Seeker read and reread passages, catharsis emerged. With each line, it became evident that the struggle against doubt permeates all aspects of existence: creative, professional, and personal. Existential questioning pressed like a weight, raising essential questions: "What is the purpose of this doubt? What truths lie beneath the surface? Where could I allow this journey to take me?"

In moments of quiet introspection, it dawned on The Seeker that many achievements are built upon the ashes of failed attempts. Yet, the stigma around failure—a concealment born within the mind—reverberated through the veins as a paralysing force. Continuously unearthing the stories of others gave The Seeker courage: artists whose first paintings were often discarded, writers who received countless rejections, entrepreneurs who started with nothing. Each narrative was a test of endurance, an embodiment of resilience against the tyranny of self-doubt.

Through reflections, it became easier to dismantle the fortress of fear—a slow process, but one punctuated with small victories. The Seeker embraced vulnerability and the strength it bred, allowing doubt to morph from an opponent to a teacher. Shadows retreated as the act of creation transformed into a sanctuary of self-exploration and acceptance.

The café, once a battleground, evolved into a fertile ground for ideas and inspiration. Each sip of coffee nourished courage, and The Seeker found solace in quiet moments. The writings expanded, each page crafted not solely in rebellion against self-doubt but as an offering, a beacon for those traversing similar paths. The words flowed like a river unyoked, inviting others to stand in solidarity against their demons. "If you, too, are held captive by the prison of doubt, know that the key lies within," The Seeker wrote. "It ignites the freedom to embrace creativity and aspiration with renewed zeal. Together, we step out of the shadows and forge a brighter path." In moments of deep reflection, The Seeker cultivated an understanding that self-doubt will always exist; it is the nature of being human. But through awareness, ownership, and creative expression, individuals can dismantle the narratives that cast long shadows. As the sun began to set beyond the café walls, The Seeker closed the journal filled with the stories and reflections of self-doubt. There lay a lingering encouragement engraved upon the final pages: "We are more than our fears, more than the limiting beliefs that cling to us. Each step taken towards understanding our own worth dismantles the prison we've built."

In essence, doubts metamorphosed into a mirror reflecting resilience. Fear became a guide, illuminating the exquisite interplay between vulnerability and strength.

The Seeker gazed outside, witnessing the world transform as dusk painted the sky with shades of gold and pink. A sense of purpose rose within, a connection formed with a community united through the struggles of doubt. The tapestry of humanity filled with vulnerabilities bled into a collective spirit—a reminder that, together, the enemy could be faced, understood, and ultimately overcome. And so, The Seeker made a promise: to step boldly into the unknown, embrace the journey, and carry forward the stories—both personal and shared—that illuminate the path towards liberation from the self-imposed prison of doubt.

Breaking Free from Chains

The journey to break free from the chains of self-doubt requires a conscious effort and a willingness to confront the thoughts and beliefs that hold us captive. This subchapter invites you to explore various techniques that not only help combat self-doubt but also empower you to reclaim your confidence and self-worth. The aim is to equip you with practical tools, exercises, affirmations, and inspiring stories of individuals who have triumphantly navigated the treacherous waters of self-doubt. To initiate your journey toward self-emancipation, it is crucial first to recognise and acknowledge the specific beliefs that contribute to your self-doubt. Often, these beliefs are rooted in past experiences, societal expectations, or internalised criticism. Begin by taking a moment to reflect on the following questions.

1. What specific areas of your life do you feel most doubtful about?

2. Where do these feelings stem from? Can you identify any past experiences or messages that have contributed to your self-doubt?

3. How have these doubts influenced your decisions and actions in the past?

Writing down your responses can serve as the first step in unearthing the sources of your self-doubt. This act of acknowledging your feelings is a powerful practice in releasing their hold on you. By articulating these experiences, you create a tangible representation of your doubts, allowing you to separate them from your self-identity.

Once you have a clearer understanding of your doubts, you can begin to confront them directly. This confrontation does not have to be a massive leap; it can start with small, manageable steps. Below are several techniques to help you navigate this process.

One powerful technique is the use of affirmations. Affirmations are positive statements that reinforce your self-worth and capabilities. They serve as reminders of your strengths and potential, combating the negative self-talk that often accompanies self-doubt. When crafting affirmations, ensure they are personal, written in the present tense, and emotionally resonant. For example: "I am capable of achieving my goals." "I trust in my abilities and instincts." "I am worthy of love and respect."

Begin by choosing a few affirmations that resonate with you. Write them down and place them where you can see them daily—on your mirror, your desk, or your phone. Recite them each day, ideally in the morning, to set a positive tone for your day. Visualisation is another effective technique that can aid in breaking free from self-doubt. Imagine yourself in a situation where you usually feel doubtful. Visualise encountering that situation with confidence and composure. Picture yourself succeeding, feeling strong and capable. This mental rehearsal can prepare your mind to embrace these positive outcomes in actual situations, gradually reducing feelings of doubt.

Additionally, consider developing a "self-empowerment toolkit." This toolkit can include a variety of resources tailored to your needs. Fill it with items that uplift you, encourage positive thinking, and foster your creativity. This may include books that inspire you, playlists filled with motivating music, quotes that resonate, or even small mementoes that remind you of your accomplishments. However, the tool that holds the most power in your toolkit is a list of past successes. Document achievements—big and small—that evoke feelings of pride and accomplishment. When self-doubt threatens to take hold, revisit this list and remind yourself of what you are capable of achieving. Connecting with a supportive community can also significantly impact your battle against self-doubt. Surround yourself with individuals who uplift and encourage you, including friends, family, or even local support groups. Seek out mentors or coaches who can provide guidance and offer validation when your inner critic becomes overbearing. Join workshops or online forums where you can share your experiences and gain perspectives from others who have walked similar paths.

These connections can provide you with the encouragement and affirmation necessary to challenge your self-doubt.

Real-world examples can inspire and show that overcoming self-doubt is possible. One notable example is J.K. Rowling, author of the Harry Potter series. Before her immense success, Rowling faced numerous rejections from publishers and a plethora of personal challenges, including unemployment and depression. However, she persisted despite her self-doubt and continued to work on her manuscript. Today, her achievements resonate worldwide, providing hope to aspiring writers everywhere. Rowling has often spoken about the importance of believing in oneself and how embracing vulnerability can lead to profound transformation.

Another inspiring story is that of Thomas Edison. Often remembered for his incredible inventions, Edison faced failure more times than he could count. He had limited formal education and was often deemed "difficult" by his teachers. Nevertheless, his unwavering belief in himself fuelled his experimentation and perseverance, ultimately leading to monumental innovations such as the electric light bulb and the phonograph. Edison's legacy serves as a timeless reminder that self-doubt is no match for determination and resilience.

As you navigate your journey, it is crucial to recognise the importance of reflection and adjustment. After implementing these techniques, take time to assess your progress. What strategies have resonated with you? Are there particular affirmations that feel more genuine than others? Allow yourself the grace to adjust your practices as needed. Self-discovery is a continual journey: be patient with yourself as you uncover what works best for you.

It's equally important to address setbacks and how to view them in the context of self-doubt. Failure does not mean you are incapable; it merely signifies a lesson learned. Embrace setbacks as opportunities for growth rather than evidence of inadequacy. Establish a mindset that promotes resilience and adaptability, ensuring that one perceived failure does not derail your entire journey.

As you grow more aware of your thoughts, those moments of doubt will transform into opportunities for reflection and growth. Harnessing the power of mindfulness can aid in this process. Mindfulness encourages you to observe your thoughts without judgment, creating a space between your feelings of doubt and your actions. Practising mindfulness techniques such as meditation, journaling, or even simple deep-breathing exercises can help you develop resilience against self-doubt.

Additionally, consider embracing the concept of "good enough." Perfectionism can often fuel self-doubt, leading us to believe we must meet unrealistic standards to be worthy of success or affection. Acknowledging that you are "good enough" as you are, flaws and all, can release you from the burdens of expectation. Celebrate your uniqueness and the gifts you bring to the table. This mindset shift can be liberating and allow you to pursue your passions without getting tangled in the web of self-imposed limitations.

Develop an accountability strategy to create a supportive framework that aligns with your aspirations. This can involve setting specific, achievable goals with deadlines and periodically reviewing your progress to ensure you stay on track. Share these goals with someone you trust who can help keep you accountable and offer encouragement along the way. This structured approach can foster a sense of purpose and ignite the motivation needed to counteract self-doubt.

We Are Our Own Enemies

Another method to combat self-doubt is to embrace lifelong learning. Continuously seeking knowledge and developing new skills not only enhances your capabilities but also serves as a counterbalance to feelings of inadequacy. Identify areas related to your goals where you feel less confident and pursue education or training in those fields. Whether through formal education, online courses, workshops, or engaging with expert content, expanding your knowledge can instil a newfound sense of confidence and agency.

In another inspiring example, consider the story of Oprah Winfrey. Faced with trauma, poverty, and discrimination, Winfrey rose above her circumstances to become a powerhouse in the media industry. Through her authenticity, resilience, and commitment to self-discovery, she has proven that our beginnings do not dictate our future. Winfrey's journey exemplifies the profound impact of overcoming self-doubt and embracing self-confidence.

As you journey toward freedom from self-doubt, remember that progress is not a linear process. Embrace the ebbs and flows of your growth. Lean on what you have learned about self-reflection and resilience. Surround yourself with reminders of your potential and take courageous steps towards your aspirations. Celebrate the small victories along the way; they are stepping stones on your path to self-emancipation.

To encapsulate your growth, commit to revisiting your self-empowerment toolkit periodically. Add to it as you discover new strategies that uplift you or seek new inspirations that resonate with your evolving self. This evolving toolkit will serve as a constant reminder that self-doubt can be dismantled piece by piece until you emerge, not only free from those chains but thriving in your authenticity.

We Are Our Own Enemies

Ultimately, the journey of breaking free from the prison of doubt is one of self-discovery and transformation. With perseverance, resilience, and a deep belief in yourself, you can build a life shaped by hope and fulfilment. As you move forward, remember that while self-doubt may linger, it does not define who you are. You possess the power to create the narrative of your life, transforming doubt into destiny.

Comfort Zones and the Illusion of Safety

The Fallacy of Comfort

In the dim light of her apartment, Sarah sat curled up on her favourite chair, a well-worn refuge of plush cushions and soft fabric. This chair, along with the familiar surroundings of her home, had become her sanctuary. She appreciated the comforting stillness of her evenings, cocooned from the world outside. Each day, she would retire to this space, surrounded by the scent of her favourite candle and the faint sound of a familiar television show, losing herself in predictable plots and reruns that provided a sense of stability. Her routines were harmlessly mundane, yet they had come to define her existence.

However, as weeks turned into months, Sarah began to notice a twinge of unease. What had once been a refuge slowly morphed into a confinement. The laughter from the sitcoms felt increasingly superficial, and a nagging sense of stagnation eclipsed the joy she derived from these routines. Gone were the days of spontaneous adventures or the thrill of meeting new people. The comfort she once cherished crept into a far more oppressive territory, becoming an invitation to doubt, resignation, and regret.

Comfort, at first glance, appears as a perfectly benign state—a sentiment cherished by many as they seek refuge from life's complexities, struggles, and uncertainties. We yearn for stability, often gravitating towards the familiar. Yet, therein lies a paradox: in our quest for comfort, we risk entrapment. The very safety we seek can become a silent prison, shackling us with invisible chains of complacency. Over time, comfort zones grow tight and constrictive, limiting our potential and stifling growth. It is essential to dissect and confront these zones for what they truly are.

Consider the story of Michael, a young professional who had invested years in a stable but unchallenging job. Initially, he was drawn to the security it provided, a steady paycheck, and predictable hours that allowed him to unwind every evening without a care. Yet, with each passing year, Michael's enthusiasm waned, replaced by a nagging sense that he was not fulfilling his potential. He watched from the sidelines as his colleagues advanced, taking bold steps toward their aspirations, while he remained in the comfort of his predictable routine. The fear of the unknown loomed large, whispering that any attempt to break free would surely fail. Thus, he remained anchored, convinced that it was safer to stay in the known, no matter how stifling it became.

However, the illusion of safety soon unveiled its darker side. The comfort zone not only stifled growth but also hindered his emotional well-being. Drifting through days that blended into one another caused Michael to experience a deeper emotional disconnection. Each time an opportunity presented itself—a chance to further his education, a request for collaboration, a potential promotion—he felt a surge of anxiety that stymied him. The prospect of change felt overwhelming, so he retreated to his chair, choosing instead to drown himself in mindless distractions.

Michael's story reflects a broader truth. Many individuals find themselves entrapped within their comfort zones, paralysed by the very fear that comfort insidiously breeds. Psychological research suggests that comfort zones can develop within a behavioural framework, wherein individuals unconsciously reinforce their avoidance of discomfort. When people engage in behaviour that is familiar and safe, they receive immediate rewards: emotional stability, peace of mind, and a temporary escape from external stressors. However, over time, these rewards do not equate to fulfilment or growth. Instead, a cycle of dependency emerges, creating an illusion that safety translates to satisfaction.

As the chill of unfulfilled desire settles in the pit of their stomach, individuals may grapple with a creeping sense of inadequacy. They often question whether they are capable of achieving goals outside their comfort zones or if they have settled for mediocrity. This internal struggle can become unbearable, leading to deep sighs of discontent and the all-too-familiar question: "Is this all there is?"

Laila, a gifted artist, faced a similar plight. Framed by the walls of her own home, filled with canvases and a cluttered workspace, she often dreamed of showcasing her art to the world. Yet, each time an opportunity arose to participate in a gallery exhibition, she hesitated. The comfort zone she created within her home, where she only painted for herself, felt both safe and restrictive. The thought of stepping into the spotlight ignited anxiety—the fear of judgment and potential failure kept her shackled. Deep down, Laila knew that to thrive as an artist, she had to expose herself to vulnerability, yet she remained imprisoned by her comfort. Instead of seeking constructive feedback or engaging with the art community, she drowned her creative frustration in painting small projects, which soon turned into more significant distractions from her aspirations.

In both Sarah and Michael's narratives, we observe a shared thread of entrapment: the protection of their comfort zones morphed into constraints that suffocated their potential. Rather than serving as vessels for growth, their spaces became stagnant pools. They illustrate a pervasive truth that comfort can be deceptive, presenting itself as a nurturing cocoon but ultimately evolving into a stifling chrysalis. The act of stepping outside one's comfort zone is daunting, yet it is crucial for genuine personal growth. This transition requires introspection and a willingness to confront fears that may initially feel insurmountable. For many, the first step is acknowledging that the comfort zone is indeed a conceptual cage. The act of self-reflection must probe deeper into the nuances of our lives. What do we fear losing by stepping out of the familiar? What potential lies dormant beneath layers of complacency?

At times, people find themselves making conscious decisions to remain in their comfort zones. This choice may stem from a rationalisation that the risk of change outweighs the potential rewards. We deceive ourselves, finding solace in the familiar while ignoring the reality that stagnation is the enemy of growth. The mind can be an architect of its prison, crafting narratives that bolster the notion of staying safe. We tell ourselves stories about the risks we are not ready to face without pausing to consider the consequences of inaction. Uncomfortably, embracing discomfort is what propels us towards transformation. David, an athletic coach, had always encouraged his team to engage in practices that pushed their limits. Yet, he found himself stuck in his own comfort zone, opting for familiar and less strenuous training methods. One fateful day, he challenged himself to participate in an extreme endurance race. As he stood at the starting line, he felt the palpable tension of the unknown gripping him. Every instinct screamed for him to retreat, back to the safety of his coaching routine, yet he took a deep breath and charged forward. The discomfort was intense, but it forced him to confront the limits he had placed upon himself. Completing that race ignited a passion and determination he had long since held at bay.

David's experience illustrates a crucial insight: confronting and embracing discomfort cultivates resilience and encourages personal growth. Each time we step outside our comfort zone, we are presented with opportunities to redefine who we are and who we might become. Seeking discomfort, immersing ourselves in challenges, or embracing vulnerability inevitably builds emotional strength. As we gather reflections about comfort zones and the illusory safety they provide, it becomes essential to reassess our own lives. Where have we settled into complacency? Are there areas of our lives—relationships, career ambitions, personal aspirations—where we are avoiding necessary risks? The answers often lie in candid self-examination, peeling back layers of dismissive rationalisations. It is also critical to recognise that the leap out of our comfort zones does not require grand gestures. Small, incremental steps can yield profound change. For Sarah, reaching out to a friend to explore an art class, rather than simply filling her evenings with television, could reignite a spark that has long been dormant. Michael might find growth by attending networking events, even if they initially evoke anxiety. Every small effort to embrace discomfort catalyses larger transformations.

The psychology of comfort zones subtly intertwines with the emotional landscape of our lives. It nudges each individual towards self-discovery, yet it demands conscious awareness. Developing a mindset attuned to recognising moments of stagnation is crucial; these moments become opportunities to challenge and redefine ourselves. In this subtle alchemy of growth, we create positive ripples that extend beyond ourselves. When we challenge our comfort zones, our actions can inspire those around us to reconsider their own limitations. Who among us has not been motivated by witnessing someone else take a brave leap? Our journeys can serve as a guiding light for others by illustrating the fulfilling possibilities that lie on the other side of discomfort. As we collectively reflect on our comfort zones, let us dare to question their necessity. When wrapped within the chains of complacency, we deny ourselves the richness of life. When we refuse to act, we stagnate not just as individuals, but as part of a broader community that flourishes upon growth, vulnerability, and shared experiences. To break free from the fallacy of comfort is not merely to step outside our sedentary routines; it is to embrace a life woven with the threads of challenge, joy, and authentic existence. The invitation is not simply to escape the prison of comfort, but to thrive in the space of possibility that lies beyond.

As we choose to reject the invitation to mediocrity, we regain agency over our lives, a power that allows for rebirth within our potential. If we remember that comfort and safety often prevent us from exploring the depths of our inner landscapes, we can learn to appreciate the discomfort that accompanies growth. It beckons us to craft a more compelling narrative, one that champions courage over fear, resilience over complacency. In doing so, the once-daunting unknown evolves into an exhilarating adventure, transforming us from prisoners of our own making into the architects of our own destinies. In the vast tapestry of existence, moments of danger, uncertainty, and the unknown are not our adversaries, but our greatest teachers. Every step taken on the verge of discomfort brings us closer to our truest selves. It's time to dismantle the fallacy of comfort, acknowledging that within each shaky step lies the power to transcend, uplift, and ultimately create a life rich in meaning and vibrancy. Reclaim the narrative of your life, challenge the limitations imposed by comfort; it begins with the realisation that only through discomfort can we truly be free.

The Call to Adventure

In the quiet stillness of a comfort zone, a sense of peace can be intoxicating. It's warm, familiar, and safe, like a soft blanket on a winter's night. But as alluring as this sanctuary may seem, it often harbours a million missed opportunities, untapped potential, and hidden dreams waiting to be realised. The comfort zone can easily become a prison if we allow it to define us, keeping us shackled in a state of stagnation as the world around us evolves and breathes with possibility.

The call to adventure invites us to step beyond that veil of comfort. It challenges us to embrace the unknown, to seek experiences that may at first appear daunting but ultimately lead to profound growth and transformation. Yet, why do so many resist this call? Fear, primarily. Fear of failure, fear of the unfamiliar, and sometimes, fear of success itself. It is a complex web woven from past disappointments, societal expectations, and the soaring barometers of self-worth that measure our every action. One might think of the hero's journey: a classic narrative found in countless stories, from ancient myths to modern movies. In this structure, a common individual is called to leave their ordinary world behind to face adventures that pit them against dragons, treacherous landscapes, and profound internal struggles. The hero doesn't initially want to leave the security of their daily routine, but a call for change pulsates beneath the surface, urging their foot towards the path scribed with uncertainty.

Just like these heroes, we too face a call to adventure that awakens our latent aspirations. It can manifest as a fleeting desire to travel, a deep-seated urge to switch careers, or simply the ambition to learn something new. What holds us back, however, is often the weight of doubt and the resistance that arises from our internal enemy—the fear of stepping away from the comfort that we have long embraced.

We Are Our Own Enemies

The Guardian, a guiding voice within each of us, interjects at this pivotal moment: "The cave you fear to enter holds the treasure you seek." This idea, brilliantly encapsulated by Joseph Campbell, speaks to the heart of the journey. The shadow of doubt looms large over our aspirations, but the very challenges we face are often stepping stones toward fulfilment. Consider someone who yearns to take their talent for photography to new heights but has restricted themselves to the familiar backdrop of their living room. They might obsessively capture the changing scenes outside their window, perfecting their skills while encased in that small, comforting world. The thought of venturing to an unfamiliar landscape evokes both excitement and paralysing fear. "What if I don't capture anything good?" or "What if I embarrass myself in front of strangers?" These internal dialogues are often the loudest voices.

However, the moment they dare to pick up their camera and step into the world, everything changes. The salty air of the ocean breeze invigorates their spirit. Every click of the shutter captures not just stunning visuals but a wealth of new experiences. Meetings with other creatives spark collaborations that had only existed in dreams. Each sunset they chase becomes a vivid palette of colours that enriches not only their portfolio but their soul. The once-feared unknown blossoms into a treasure trove of creativity and connection.

This is where the interjection of hope becomes vital. The Guardian whispers gently, "Do not be afraid to give up the good to go for the great." Perhaps comfort has lulled you into complacency, but the potential is endless just beyond your door. It could be that career pivot you hesitate to take, the art class you dream of enrolling in, or the relationship you long to rekindle but fear facing the past.

We Are Our Own Enemies

Through the lens of adventure, we can redefine our self-imposed barriers. Picture this: a young woman, Lisa, who has always been the shyest in her circle. She has a flair for cooking, but keeps her culinary prowess confined to family dinners and her close-knit circle of friends. A wave of discontent washes over her when she discovers a local cooking competition. Images of herself failing or stumbling on stage gnaw at her resolve. Yet, somewhere deep within, excitement flickers like a long-dormant flame.

One evening, propelled by that flicker, she decides to sign up. The adrenaline rush is both thrilling and terrifying. The first day of the competition arrives, and her heart pounds with each step she takes toward the venue. The fear is palpable... what if she embarrasses herself? But as she steps into the kitchen, the familiar scent of spices and the warm glow of searing pans envelop her like a second skin. She feels alive, ignited by the challenge. As the competition unfolds, she stumbles on a few dishes but manages to recover. The judges' feedback becomes an opportunity for growth rather than a damning verdict. By the end of the journey, she doesn't win first place, but with every round, Lisa discovers her voice, her style, and a newfound confidence that ripples into every aspect of her life. From that moment on, she no longer confines her talents to the shadows of complacency but instead takes bold steps toward her dreams.

The Guardian reminds us: "The more you give, the more you receive." The adventure isn't merely about the pursuit of accolades or successes; it is about who we become in the process. Transcending our comfort zones doesn't mean abandoning all we know; it means expanding our horizons and embracing the vastness of our potential.

We Are Our Own Enemies

Transformation does not happen overnight; it is a series of small, audacious decisions that propel us into the unknown. First comes the recognition, a sense that something is amiss in the comfort of routine. Then, an acknowledgement of that inner voice urging us to explore. This leads to a commitment, a defining moment where we consciously decide to pursue adventure and not let fear stifle our aspirations.

But beyond commitment lies action. Action rekindles fire and breathes life into stagnant dreams. If the call to adventure were to manifest as a physical place, it would be bustling with possibility—throngs of people engaged in lively discussion, laughter bubbling forward, and a sense of camaraderie echoing in the air. Each interaction, each new idea is a stepping stone, laying a foundation upon which eventual triumphs build.

We must remember that the call to adventure is not a solitary journey; it is a communal experience. We are surrounded by fellow travellers on their quests for growth and fulfilment. When we step out of our comfort zone, we influence those around us, inviting them to join us or inspiring them to pursue their own daring endeavours.

In a world where many remain shackled by their fears, those who embark on adventures become beacons of possibility. Each story shared, every challenge faced, is a thread woven into the collective tapestry of our human experience. The courage to venture forth ignites a ripple effect; imagine a group of friends pushing each other to take that leap, whether it's starting a business, climbing a mountain, or pursuing a passion project. As they encourage one another, doubts dissipate in the shared enthusiasm and collective resolve.

On this journey, it's crucial to cultivate a support system that empowers us to pursue our desires boldly. Find that circle of influence, a network of people who uplift you and challenge your limitations, celebrating victories while providing stability when faced with setbacks. The Guardian reminds us: "Surround yourself with only people who are going to lift you higher." So, whether your adventure involves starting a film project, writing your first novel, or speaking at a conference, let go of the bonds of doubt and embrace the wonders that await you. Each brave decision chips away at the illusion created by comfort, revealing a vibrant palette of experiences and connections.

Take actionable steps toward the journey that beckons you. Start small; even the tiniest action can create a massive ripple effect. Say yes to that invitation to try a new class. Join that local group that shares your interests, or start a journal to articulate your dreams. The key is taking consistent action leading to growth.

Explore the uncharted territories of your aspirations. Within each leap beyond our comfort zone lies the potential for remarkable change, tales worth telling, and an expansive view of what's possible. The unmarked paths await brave souls willing to embrace uncertainty and forge ahead.

In closing, the call to adventure is more than a challenge; it is an invitation to embrace life in its fullest spectrum. A chance to transcend limitations, shed the past, and align with the dreamer within. It transforms fear into fuel, propelling us toward our unique destinies.

As the Guardian imparts one final thought: "Life begins at the edge of your comfort zone." Let that be the rallying cry as you embark on your adventure, fully aware that just beyond lies an existence far greater than what is familiar. Answer the call, for the world awaits the brilliance that is uniquely yours.

Testing Boundaries

Stepping outside of our comfort zones can feel like embarking on a daunting journey, fraught with uncertainty and potential discomfort. Yet, it is through these very experiences that we discover our true selves and the boundless possibilities that lie beyond the familiar. In this section, we will engage in a series of practical exercises, guided by the metaphorical figure of The Guardian, who serves as both protector and challenger. The aim is to provide a structured means for readers to explore new experiences, thereby illustrating the vast benefits of embracing vulnerability.

The Guardian encourages us to recognise that each boundary we encounter—be it emotional, mental, or physical—can be tested and transformed into opportunities for growth. With intentionality, we can embrace challenges that expand our horizons and redefine what we believe is possible.

As we embark on these exercises, keep in mind that each step outside your comfort zone does not need to resemble a grand leap; sometimes, small shifts can yield profound results. The Guardian reminds us that the growth journey often begins with a single, deliberate step. Let us begin with foundational exercises designed to broaden your comfort zone gradually.

The first exercise invites you to assess your current comfort zones. Take a moment to reflect on the areas of your life where you feel most secure and the aspects that elicit discomfort or anxiety. Consider your daily routines, relationships, and aspirations. Write down three specific comfort zones you identify, paired with three corresponding fears or hesitations that keep you from exploring beyond those boundaries. This exercise serves as a way to acknowledge and name the limitations you currently face.

We Are Our Own Enemies

Once you have completed this assessment, The Guardian would encourage you to resist the urge to view these comfort zones as permanent fixtures. Instead, think of them as temporary shelters that can be expanded. For your next challenge, choose one of the identified comfort zones and set an intention to step outside of it within the next week.

For instance, if you identified social interactions as a comfort zone, consider intentionally engaging with a new social group or participating in an event where you may not know anyone. If your boundaries exist in the realm of your career, contemplate taking on a task or project that feels slightly intimidating yet intriguing. The key here is to choose a challenge that feels accessible but still requires you to stretch your limits.

As you commit to this challenge, outline the steps you will take to ensure its success. Create an action plan that includes specific dates, potential obstacles, and strategies to overcome those obstacles. By mapping out your journey, you engage The Guardian in a cooperative endeavour toward exploration.

Another powerful exercise involves cultivating curiosity. The Guardian invites you to approach life with a beginner's mindset, fostering openness to new experiences. Consider dedicating a week to exploring something you have always been curious about but never pursued. It could be taking a cooking class, joining a book club, or even trying a new physical activity, such as rock climbing or yoga. As you delve into this new experience, take notes on how you feel, the challenges you face, and the insights you gain.

Curiosity often serves as a pathway to vulnerability, allowing us to encounter unfamiliar situations with a sense of wonder rather than apprehension. As you embark on this week of exploration, keep The Guardian in mind as an ally; visualise them encouraging you to embrace any moments of discomfort, viewing them as opportunities for growth.

In the spirit of vulnerability, consider incorporating an "Accountability Partner" into your journey. This individual can be a friend, family member, or colleague who shares similar desires to push their boundaries. Together, you can establish a list of mutual goals and challenges to tackle over a set period—perhaps a month.

Each week, check in with each other to share your experiences, challenges faced, and lessons learned. This partnership not only fosters accountability but also creates a supportive space where both parties can celebrate one another's victories, however small they may seem. The Guardian stands alongside you in this endeavour, ensuring you understand that true connection and growth often arise from shared experiences.

As you continue to explore and tackle challenges, it's crucial to reflect on your progress. Maintaining a journal dedicated to your findings can be a valuable tool in this process. Each time you step outside your comfort zone, take a moment to jot down your emotions, thoughts, and any insights that emerge. What fears did you confront? What unexpected successes did you encounter? How did these experiences shift your perspective of self or the world around you?

The act of journaling not only provides clarity but also serves as a chronicle of your transformation. You may discover recurring themes that reveal deeper-seated beliefs about yourself, guiding you further in your journey of self-discovery. The Guardian, ever watchful, encourages you to embrace this reflective practice and revisit your entries over time to recognise how far you've come.

As your comfort zone expands, consider heightening the stakes with more challenging exercises. One such exercise involves public speaking. Many individuals harbour a significant fear of speaking in front of an audience. The Guardian prompts you to confront this fear head-on. Choose a topic you are passionate about, and draft a short presentation. Seek opportunities to present this material to a small group, whether it's at a local meetup, a community event, or even among friends and family. As you prepare, practice the art of visualising success. Imagine delivering your speech with confidence, captivating your audience's attention. Visualisation can serve as a powerful tool to alleviate anxiety, allowing you to step into the experience with greater boldness.

In tandem with public speaking, another exercise invites you to engage in something that requires you to ask for help. This could range from simple tasks, such as requesting assistance at a café or striking up a conversation with someone new, to more complex endeavours, like seeking guidance on a complex project. Asking for help often challenges our egos and pushes us out of our comfort zones. As you engage in these exercises, remind yourself of the synergy between vulnerability and growth. The Guardian encourages you to remember that asking for help does not signify weakness but rather courage. Embracing discomfort often leads to unexpected wisdom and deeper connections, fostering a more profound understanding of ourselves and those around us.

Throughout this journey, it is essential to maintain a compassionate mindset. The Guardian serves as a poignant reminder that kindness toward oneself is paramount when navigating the challenges of growth and expansion. With every misstep or fear that causes you to falter, acknowledge those feelings without judgment. Understand that growth is a process, a series of moments rather than a singular achievement.

We Are Our Own Enemies

Incorporating moments of self-care and celebration is vital. After completing a challenging exercise or particularly daunting task, take a moment to celebrate your accomplishments and reflect on the lessons you've learned. Perhaps treat yourself to a Movie Night, go for a spa day, or enjoy a nature excursion. Celebrating even the tiniest victories reinforces the positive association with stepping outside of your comfort zone.

A transformative exercise to consider is the commitment to "Embrace Discomfort." Challenge yourself to do one uncomfortable thing each day for a month. This might mean saying "yes" to opportunities you would typically decline, taking a cold shower, or striking up a conversation with a stranger. With each deliberate and calculated act of discomfort, The Guardian walks alongside you, encouraging you to witness how these experiences contribute to the expansion of your capabilities and confidence. As you navigate through these daily challenges, remain attuned to your feelings and reactions. What fears arise? What moments bring about exhilaration or dread? Keep track of these occurrences in your journal, as they'll lend insight into your patterns of behaviour and offer a deeper understanding of the roots of your comfort zones.

Building upon your experiences, consider experimenting with the concept of 'Micro-Adventures.' The Guardian invites you to look for ways to infuse more adventure into your daily life, even in small, manageable ways. This might mean taking a new route to work, visiting a new café, or participating in a local activity you've never tried before. These micro-adventures can lead to significant shifts in perspective and foster feelings of excitement and possibility. The Guardian encourages exploration and spontaneity, helping you uncover experiences that foster creativity, joy, and connection to the world around you.

We Are Our Own Enemies

As you advance further along this transformative path, you may find that your newly expanded comfort zone invites you to redefine your goals and aspirations. Anticipate that some of these challenges will propel you toward new dreams that may have once felt unattainable. Take time to dream big. The Guardian suggests crafting a vision board that reflects your newfound aspirations and desires inspired by your experiences. Collect images, quotes, and ideas that resonate with you and construct a visual representation of the possibilities that lie ahead.

Finally, as you complete this journey of testing boundaries and exploring the unknown, remember that stepping outside your comfort zone is not a destination but a lifelong journey. The Guardian remains a steadfast partner by your side, continuously advocating for courageous exploration and guiding you to confront each new boundary as it arises. In closing, the path of growth stretches infinitely before you, fuelled by the courage to embrace discomfort, seek vulnerability, and engage intentionally with the world. Remain open to the lessons learned and experiences gained, for they will enrich not only your journey but also the lives of those around you. The true power of testing boundaries lies in discovering the strength within, transforming fear into action, and ultimately becoming your own greatest ally in life's adventure.

Procrastination: Tomorrow's Greatest Thief

The Lure of Delay

The Seeker stands at the precipice of possibility, the horizon shimmering with potential, yet finds themselves ensnared in a web of hesitation and self-doubt. While the world around them buzzes with activity and ambition, they linger in a space where time is both an ally and an adversary. The seductive lull of procrastination, that seemingly benign indulgence in delay, whispers promisingly in their ear, creating a false sense of security that tomorrow will surely be a better day for action.

In these quiet moments, the Seeker grapples with the weight of their aspirations, the dreams that flicker like distant stars in the night sky. Each desire—whether it's to pursue a career, a creative endeavour, or a personal transformation—exists as a potential path forward. Yet, procrastination clouds their vision, transforming promises of future achievement into mere shadows that elude their grasp with each passing day. The initial thrill of ambition fades, replaced by the heavy blanket of complacency, and the Seeker finds their dreams at odds with the monotony of daily life.

The allure of delay is complex, unfolding through a combination of psychological and emotional factors. Central to this phenomenon is a desire for immediate gratification, a powerful driver that pulls the Seeker away from long-term goals. In the short term, opting for comfort over discomfort feels rewarding. Scrolling through social media, binge-watching a favourite series, or engaging in mindless tasks become instant escapes from the anxiety of tackling life's big challenges. These are brief highs that reinforce the procrastination habit, making it difficult to pivot towards action.

Underneath this immediate gratification lies a fear—an ever-present adversary lurking in the shadows of the Seeker's mind. The fear of failure and the fear of success create a paradox that stifles progress. The Seeker clings to the familiar, dreading the risk of stepping into the unknown. Failure casts a long shadow, highlighting insecurities and past disappointments that loom large in their self-perception. Similarly, the fear of success, a less discussed but equally potent force, becomes a barrier to moving forward. The implications of growth, levels of responsibility, and the fear of losing one's identity can be daunting, leading the Seeker to retreat into delay. The psychology of procrastination is also rooted in perfectionism. Perhaps the Seeker has lofty standards, with initiative built on visions of flawlessly executing their dreams. Each time they contemplate action, the voice of perfectionism chimes in, sowing seeds of doubt. "If you can't do it perfectly, then why do it at all?" it taunts. As the Seeker becomes paralysed by the prospect of not measuring up, they succumb to procrastination's grip. The time that could be spent polishing ideas or taking steps toward goals instead gets lost in a cycle of over-analysis and hesitation.

Connection also plays a crucial role in understanding procrastination. The Seeker may carry childhood memories marked by external expectations or conditions for approval—instances that might condition them to hesitate for fear of not meeting the standards set by others. As adults, these memories can translate into social anxiety, causing the Seeker to postpone endeavours that require stepping out into the world where judgment and validation await. An immediate need for acceptance overshadows the promised joy of pursuing personal aspirations.

We Are Our Own Enemies

Moreover, procrastination thrives on self-identity. The Seeker may subconsciously grapple with their sense of self-worth. They may adopt narratives that paint them as "lazy" or "unmotivated," trapping them in a negative feedback loop. Each delay reinforces these beliefs; with every unfulfilled intention, their self-image deteriorates. This cycle creates a deep-seated conflict, pitting the Seeker's desires against the stories they tell themselves, a battle that seemingly favours the adversary, procrastination.

In this exploration of the nature of procrastination, it becomes clear that it is not simply about delaying tasks but is a rich tapestry woven with the threads of emotion, motivation, fear, and identity. The Seeker often carries the weight of both personal narratives and societal expectations on their shoulders, making the act of overcoming procrastination feel monumental. Even the smallest of aspirations can feel like a daunting mountain when faced with the relentless tide of self-doubt.

As the Seeker wrestles with these realities, it becomes essential to shine a light on hope—the flicker of possibility that exists alongside these struggles. Acknowledging the seductive nature of procrastination is a brave first step. Armed with the knowledge of its psychological underpinnings, they can begin to fight back against the enemy that lurks within.

The first tactic in this journey is developing self-awareness. The Seeker must learn to recognise the urges and signs of procrastination as they emerge. Building mindfulness can illuminate the moments where the choice to delay occurs. Rather than becoming engulfed by the all-consuming guilt of inaction, they can foster curiosity about their behaviours. Questions such as "What am I terrified of?" or "What beliefs are influencing this hesitation?" create opportunities for reflection and personal growth. Building a strategy to tackle procrastination also requires redefining what success means. The Seeker must confront the toxic pressure of perfectionism that hinders their progress. By embracing the idea that some steps taken imperfectly are better than pursuing an unattainable standard, they unlock a path forward. Small, incremental actions replace grand gestures, creating a sense of momentum that feels attainable and meaningful.

In cultivating resilience and self-compassion, the Seeker learns to forgive themselves for past delays. The process of tackling procrastination involves facing discomfort head-on and recognising that setbacks are an inevitable part of the journey. A slip into procrastination doesn't warrant self-condemnation; instead, it provides a valuable opportunity to reassess motivations and strategies. Additionally, the Seeker can find grounding in the practice of goal-setting, utilising tools such as actionable plans and accountability measures. Breaking down dreams into manageable tasks transforms daunting ambitions into tangible, bite-sized pieces. The act of checking off completed tasks becomes a motivator, forging a connection between effort and achievement.

Peer support and community engagement can further aid the Seeker in overcoming procrastination. Sharing aspirations with trusted friends or like-minded individuals creates a network of accountability. The act of vocalising dreams brings them into the realm of shared reality, amplifying the desire to act. Communities that champion collective growth encourage, celebrating each small victory in a space free from judgment.

In essence, the Seeker's struggle with procrastination highlights the complexities of the human experience. Each moment of delay serves as an invitation to heroism—the heroism of confronting fears, challenging narratives about self-worth, and dismantling the barriers created by past experiences. As they rise against the enemy within, the Seeker finds themselves not only reclaiming their dreams but also discovering their strength in vulnerability. The pursuit of transformation is not a solitary journey; it necessitates courage and an understanding that discomfort is a prelude to growth. For every moment spent delaying action, there exists the possibility of engaging with the deeper richness of life. The path may be fraught with challenges, but within it lies a profound truth: the Seeker possesses the innate ability to forge their way forward. With each step taken against procrastination, they inch closer to realising the dreams that once felt just beyond reach. In the grand tapestry of existence, where moments intermingle and intertwine, the Seeker finds that the power to transcend delay is not merely about ambition; it is about embracing the self. It is an act of reclamation: turning the lens inward to discover the parts of themselves that have been overshadowed by doubt. The journey promises not just accomplishments but the chance to forge an authentic relationship with time and potential.

As the Seeker stands ready to embark upon this journey, they recognise that the enemy within can become their greatest teacher. Procrastination, initially perceived as a thief of dreams, transforms into a catalyst for profound self-discovery. By understanding its seductive nature and unravelling the complexities of their emotional landscape, the Seeker learns to navigate the labyrinth of their aspirations with newfound clarity. In doing so, they find that the journey is as vital as the destination, a reflection of a life lived in pursuit of authenticity rather than mere accomplishment. With each passing day, the temptation to delay may still exist; however, the Seeker is equipped with insights that illuminate their path. They learn that courage is not the absence of fear or hesitance but the determination to act despite it. What once felt like a burden of procrastination morphs into an opportunity for growth, inviting the Seeker to explore new dimensions of their being. In this way, they become the architects of their own futures, crafting lives characterised by passion, purpose, and, ultimately, fulfilment. This power to overcome the lure of delay is a gift—the gift of agency, enabling the Seeker to reclaim their dreams from tomorrow, crafting a narrative rooted in action and intention. The delicate interplay of ambition and introspection shapes their reality, urging them to engage with life authentically and boldly. This transformation stands as a testament to the truth within the overarching theme of our collective struggle: we are our own enemies, yet we are also our own saviours. Each day marks a new opportunity to rise against procrastination, to choose to embrace the journey over the destination, and to sow the seeds of our dreams unfettered by the chains of delay.

Strategies for Action

In the landscape of personal growth, procrastination often lies in wait, like a predator, ready to snuff out dreams before they can even take flight. It thrives in the shadows of doubt and fear, whispering seductive promises that tomorrow will be the perfect day to start. Yet, we know too well that tomorrow can easily morph into next week, next month, or even next year. To reclaim our time and achieve our goals, we must equip ourselves with effective strategies to combat this omnipresent thief. The following sections will outline comprehensive techniques ranging from time management and prioritisation to mindfulness practices, all designed to foster proactive engagement with our aspirations.

To navigate the realm of procrastination, we first need to understand what propels it. The causes are often deeply embedded within our emotional and cognitive landscapes. Fear of failure, perfectionism, and feeling overwhelmed can all serve as catalysts for procrastination. By identifying these triggers, we can tailor our strategies to address them directly, enabling us to take the first crucial steps toward action.

One effective approach to mitigating procrastination is through the use of time-management techniques. Time is our most precious resource, and managing it wisely allows us to use it effectively. Calendar tools and traditional planners have evolved into sophisticated apps that help allocate our time effectively. Utilising these tools starts with blocking out specific chunks of time dedicated to individual tasks. For instance, the Pomodoro Technique encourages working in short bursts, typically 25 minutes, followed by a five-minute break. This method helps maintain focus by creating mini-deadlines around each task, transforming work into manageable segments that feel less daunting.

Moreover, establishing a routine can provide structure and stability to our daily activities. By designating specific times for certain tasks, we create an environment where action becomes habitual. The brain thrives on consistency; when we repeatedly assign time slots for particular activities, we signal to ourselves that these tasks are a priority. For example, if writing a novel is a goal, dedicating an hour every morning to writing without distractions lays the foundation for consistent progress. Prioritisation is another indispensable strategy in our fight against procrastination. The Eisenhower Matrix, a popular tool for prioritising tasks, categorises them based on urgency and importance. By distinguishing between what is urgent and what is important, we can focus our energy on activities that genuinely contribute to our long-term goals. For instance, a task may feel urgent if it has an approaching deadline, but it may not align with our larger aspirations. Being aware of this distinction helps us allocate our time and resources more wisely, ensuring we are not merely busy but effectively working toward our objectives.

A practical example of prioritisation comes from a story of a young woman named Maya, who struggled to balance work, school, and personal projects. Each day, she was overwhelmed by the multitude of tasks vying for her attention. She began using the Eisenhower Matrix, creating a visual representation of her responsibilities. Over time, she learned to delegate less important tasks to others or postpone them, and she allocated her time mostly to the work that propelled her towards her long-term goals. Ultimately, she graduated with honours and launched a successful small business, all because she learned to prioritise her commitments effectively.

Mindfulness practices further enhance our ability to combat procrastination by aligning our mindsets with our goals. The act of mindfulness encourages present-focusing and clarity, drawing our awareness to the tasks at hand rather than future worries or past mistakes. Techniques such as meditation can help cultivate a focused mindset, allowing us to break free from the cycle of overthinking, which often leads to inaction.

Start the day with a few minutes of mindfulness meditation, allowing your mind to settle. Focus on your breath, letting each inhale instil motivation while releasing the stress that often fuels procrastination with each exhale. In this state of presence, visualise the goals you wish to achieve and the steps needed to reach them. This grounding practice not only reduces anxiety but also fosters a sense of confidence that propels us into action.

Integrating mindfulness into daily routines does not require a significant time commitment. Short pauses throughout the day can help deepen awareness and prevent feelings of overwhelm. Take a moment to step away from your desk during long work hours. Stretch, breathe deeply, and reconnect with your body. This brief interlude can recharge your mental batteries, allowing you to return to your tasks with renewed vigour.

Another powerful technique grounded in mindfulness is the practice of gratitude. By acknowledging and appreciating even the smallest accomplishments, we shift our focus away from what we have yet to achieve. Maintaining a gratitude journal can encourage this mindset. At the end of each day, devote a few minutes to writing down three things you accomplished, no matter how small. Over time, this simple habit builds momentum, reinforcing a positive feedback loop that spurs further action.

As we delve deeper into the strategies for action, let's explore the concept of accountability. In sharing our goals with others, we not only create a support network but also amplify our commitment. When we vocalise our aspirations, we solidify them in a way that transforms them from abstract concepts into tangible realities.

Consider forming or joining an accountability group. These are small collectives of individuals who check in with one another, sharing progress toward their respective goals. The structure of regular meetings, whether weekly or bi-weekly, not only establishes a framework for monitoring progress but also fosters an environment of support and encouragement. Knowing that others are invested in our success can be an incredibly powerful motivator, as it transforms personal goals into collective efforts that are simultaneously shared.

Particularly moving is the story of Jason, who endeavoured to write a memoir. For years, he put off the task, convinced he lacked the time and skills. Eventually, he joined a writing group where members shared ongoing projects and deadlines. The gentle nudges from fellow writers ignited a fire within him, shifting his perspective on the endeavour from daunting to manageable. With their encouragement, he finally committed to writing, and his memoir, which felt like a distant dream for so long, became a published work.

Next, let's discuss the importance of setting specific and achievable goals, commonly referred to as SMART goals: Specific, Measurable, Achievable, Relevant, and Time-bound. When goals are articulated in this manner, they feel less nebulous, allowing for focused action steps. For instance, rather than saying, "I want to get fit," a SMART goal would state, "I will go for a 30-minute run every morning at 7 AM, five times a week." This precise formulation clarifies expectations and lays out a roadmap, transforming an intimidating ambition into attainable actions.

Conversely, avoid overwhelming yourself with excessive goals. The art of limitation is a strategy to encompass; being realistic about what can be achieved within designated time frames is crucial. Focus on quality over quantity. By concentrating your efforts on fewer, high-impact goals, you can cultivate a deeper sense of fulfilment in each accomplished task.

The idea of visualisation is another technique that leverages the power of the mind to combat procrastination. Visualise not only the result but the steps needed to reach it. Create a vivid mental image of achieving your goal, paying attention to the emotions, sensations, and environments that accompany success. This vivid imagery can energise you in moments of doubt or lethargy, providing a reminder of why you started in the first place.

Let's return to our friend Maya for an exploration of visualisation. After mastering her time management and prioritisation skills, she took it a step further by creating a vision board. On a poster board, she collected images, quotes, and affirmations that represented her dreams and aspirations, from her desire to own a successful business to her vision of a balanced personal life. Every morning, she spent a few moments reflecting on her vision board, which helped keep her motivated and reminded her of her ultimate goals.

Another fascinating strategy for battling procrastination involves "temptation bundling." This technique pairs tasks that may seem tedious with activities that bring joy. It capitalises on the principle of reinforcement, allowing you to harness enjoyable elements while tackling less appealing tasks. For instance, if you dread folding laundry, pair it with listening to your favourite podcast or enjoying a great audiobook. By intertwining tasks, you can foster a sense of reward, encouraging you to take action.

Building upon this, let's also acknowledge the significance of environmental design. Our surroundings significantly influence our behaviour, and creating an environment conducive to productivity is crucial. This could mean decluttering our workspace to minimise distractions, using apps that limit online interruptions, or even curating a playlist that motivates us while we work. By architecting an environment that supports focus and engagement, we increase our likelihood of overcoming procrastination.

The story of an artist named Leah exemplifies this strategy. She found herself continually distracted by social media while working on her latest piece. To counteract this, she decided to limit her time on her devices. Leah created a dedicated studio space filled with inspiring art, natural light, and minimal distractions. Each time she entered this space, she felt a surge of creativity that propelled her forward, ultimately resulting in an art exhibition that showcased her relentless passion.

We Are Our Own Enemies

Finally, it's crucial to maintain a mindset of self-compassion. Perfectionism is an enemy of action; it often leads to paralysing fears that hold us captive in a cycle of procrastination. Embrace the idea that progress, not perfection, is the ultimate goal. Allow yourself to make mistakes, as they are a part of the learning process. Understanding that self-worth is not contingent upon flawless execution can liberate the mind and foster resilience.

In practising self-compassion, also acknowledge that setbacks and moments of procrastination happen to all of us. Rather than becoming frustrated or defeated, gently redirect your focus back toward your goals. This dynamic self-talk not only reinforces a growth mindset but also cultivates a nurturing relationship with oneself, one that fosters continued growth despite obstacles.

Equipped with these strategies, the journey forward becomes increasingly navigable. By implementing time management techniques, enhancing prioritisation skills, embracing mindfulness practices, seeking accountability, and fostering self-compassion, we create an intricate web of support that empowers proactive engagement with our dreams.

As we carve a path through the dense underbrush of procrastination, remember that the journey is as essential as the destination. The act of taking immediate action on our aspirations creates momentum, which can be the very force that breaks the cycle of inaction and fear. With intention and commitment, we all possess the power to conquer procrastination and align our lives with our fullest potential.

Ultimately, the legacy of our lives will be defined by the actions we choose to take today, rather than what we postpone for tomorrow. It is within our power to transform our goals into achievements, to silence the whispers of procrastination with each triumphant step forward. Let's take those steps together, transforming fear into action and dreams into reality, one strategy at a time.

Negative Self-Talk and the Inner Critic

Voices We Inherit

The weight of words can shift the trajectory of a life, often without us fully understanding their origin. Every human being grapples with an inner voice—a dialogue that shapes our perceptions, influences our decisions, and moulds our self-worth. However, many are unaware that external sources, including family, friends, culture, and society often influence the tone and content of this internal commentator. In this exploration of negative self-talk, we will delve into the origins of these voices, unravelling the threads that connect our past experiences to the critical dialogues we engage in with ourselves today.

Growing up in a small town, I often found myself ensnared in the web of comparison that wove through my childhood. The whispers of my peers echoed in my mind—ill-fated judgments based on my performance in sports, my appearance, or even my choice of friends. Each comment, however seemingly innocent, laid a brick in the wall of my self-doubt. My mother's well-meaning yet critical words about my grades felt like daggers when they silently articulated, "You're not smart enough." The impact of those moments still reverberates, surfacing in conversations I have with myself during times of uncertainty.

As we begin to trace the sources of our negative self-talk, it's essential to recognise that these voices do not just originate from the present. They are often echoes of our formative years. The tone of a parent's voice, filled with disappointment or impatience, can implant seeds of self-criticism that flourish into a garden of discontent. My father's harsh reprimands for minor failures instilled in me a belief that perfection was not only desirable but also necessary. Even today, that pressure manifests when I hesitate to take risks or express creativity, fearful of falling short once again.

In psychological terms, this phenomenon is often explained through the lens of social learning theory. Proposed by Albert Bandura, this theory emphasises the role of observation in influencing behaviour and beliefs. From a young age, we witness the reactions of those around us—parents, teachers, and friends—and internalise these responses as our own. If we observe someone criticising themselves or reacting negatively to their perceived shortcomings, we may unconsciously adopt those same patterns of self-talk. This voiceless classroom of life becomes a breeding ground for critical thinking that, over time, transforms into debilitating self-talk.

I remember vividly standing in front of the bathroom mirror, preparing for a school presentation. My stomach churned with anxicty as I practised my speech repeatedly, only to hear my mother's quiet yet persistent voice in my ear: "Don't embarrass yourself." I felt the familiar knot of self-doubt tighten around me, paralysing my confidence. My reflection showed a child longing for approval, yet all I could hear was the insistent murmur of my inner critic, fuelled by those external voices. It is in moments like this that we begin to see how deeply intertwined our self-perception is with the external stimuli we have experienced.

Through years of engagement with psychological literature, I discovered a robust concept called the 'inner critic,' highlighted by experts such as Dr Richard Schwartz and his development of Internal Family Systems (IFS) therapy. Schwartz describes the inner critic as an internalised protector, one that emerged from childhood experiences to shield us from perceived threats or failures. This protector, however, often assumes the role of a tyrant, creating a narrative steeped in self-doubt and harsh judgment. Dr Kristin Neff's work on self-compassion suggests that this inner critic can be quelled through kindness and understanding toward oneself, allowing individuals to dismantle the damaging effects of inherited negative self-talk.

The exploration of self-talk often introduces us to further complexities, such as the impact of cultural values and societal expectations. Growing up in a community that placed immense value on success and high achievement, I absorbed the notion that anything less than perfection was unacceptable. This societal pressure became a significant voice in my inner dialogue, feeding my anxiety and amplifying my fears of failure. I noticed this not just in myself but reflected across my peers—an entire generation raised on the belief that only through relentless striving could one carve out their worth.

In juxtaposition, my friends who experienced more supportive family dynamics seemed to communicate with themselves more compassionately. They had inherited voices that echoed encouragement and resilience rather than criticism. Psychologists agree that self-talk is closely linked to the narratives we construct about our lives, which in turn influence our varying degrees of self-esteem and life satisfaction. This disparity in our inner dialogues highlights the powerful influence of inherited voices, as well as our capacity for change.

The battle against negative self-talk is not merely a personal endeavour; it encompasses familial and communal realms. To illustrate this, I recall my friend Sarah. Open and warm, she approached life with a sense of joy and adventure. However, lurking beneath her cheerful exterior was a critical voice that whispered distressing reminders of past missteps. Whenever an opportunity arose—a new job, a relationship, or a creative endeavour—she would almost instinctively retreat into self-criticism, echoing comments she had heard throughout her life: "You'll fail like you always do," or "Why would anyone want to choose you?" As we approached her anxieties together, it became increasingly clear that the origin of Sarah's inner critic was multifaceted. Her parents, while loving, had instilled a belief that any slip would bring shame to the family. The culmination of schoolyard teasing and remarks from authority figures had deepened this belief in her own inadequacies, creating an avalanche of self-critical commentary.

When I asked her about her self-talk, she struggled to articulate how it felt. I openly shared my own struggles with negative self-talk, which surprisingly opened a doorway for her to explore her feelings further. This reciprocal honesty prematurely dissolved the oppressive atmosphere that had been wrapped around her insecurities. Through carefully examining her inherited narratives, Sarah began to deconstruct the threads of criticism and absurd standards imposed by her childhood experiences and societal expectations.

In psychological frameworks, this kind of exploration is often interwoven with a therapeutic concept known as 'cognitive restructuring.' It involves identifying negative thoughts and beliefs, challenging their validity, and ultimately replacing them with healthier and more constructive alternatives. As Sarah began to engage in this thought challenge, her language underwent a transformation. Instead of "I will fail," she started expressing, "I will give it a try," or "I deserve this opportunity." This simple shift, reminiscent of the tactics outlined by cognitive-behavioural therapy, began to bolster her self-image and diminish the power of her inner critic.

The energy behind our inherited voices often comes from a desire for protection or understanding. When we experience voices that chastise us, we often face an underlying fear of abandonment, failure, or judgment. Recognising this connection is key to understanding why we silence ourselves. Experiencing the daunting nature of criticism leads us to succumb to our inner critics, as we instinctively prepare ourselves for future harm. Researchers suggest that understanding this connection can cultivate self-awareness and help individuals respond to their inner critic with resilience rather than resignation.

As we explore these themes further, we encounter not only personal stories but broader societal dynamics that expose how public discourse influences our inner dialogues. Cultures steeped in unrealistic standards—such as beauty, success, and intelligence—perpetuate cycles of discontent and internal punishment. Social media platforms, once lauded as spaces for connection, have morphed into arenas of relentless comparison. The influence of these platforms serves to magnify our insecurities, replacing voices of complexity with a cacophony of fear and inadequacy.

In reflecting on my journey, I found myself drawn to the concept of 'cognitive dissonance.' The discomfort experienced when our beliefs clash with our self-perception often fuels negative self-talk. Social media, riddled with curated versions of reality, presents us with unattainable ideals, and in comparison, our own lives can feel irretrievably flawed. The voices we inherit from societal standards often feel insurmountable—further entwining us in the cycle of self-doubt and harsh internal criticism.

We Are Our Own Enemies

Breaking free from these inherited voices involves a commitment to intentionally cultivate a new inner narrative. We must learn to be the authors of our own dialogues, gradually peeling back the layers of inherited criticism while nurturing the seeds of encouragement and self-compassion. I remember the first time I consciously applied this practice: standing before the mirror, I chose to speak kindly to myself, regaling a story of resilience rather than defeat. "You are capable," I said, "and you have survived much worse." It felt foreign, but over time, this practice became a lifeline, a new voice emerging from within, free from the confines of inherited disapproval.

Engaging fully in this process requires patience, vulnerability, and resilience. It asks for the courage to challenge long-standing narratives and the willingness to discover new voices that serve our well-being. As we step away from inherited voices, we may also find community—those who share similar battles, those who have shattered their negative self-talk and replaced it with empathy and understanding.

Today, let us embrace our stories, our voices, and the courage to reshape our inner dialogue. No longer must we allow the echoes of our past to dictate our present. Instead, let those voices fade softly into background noise as we create a new rhythm of self-affirmation and resilience, one that honours our journey and celebrates our progress.

With intention and practice, we can begin to dismantle the barriers erected by inherited voices, moving toward an authentic and compassionate relationship with ourselves. Our inner dialogue holds the power to either forge a path fraught with barriers or illuminate a journey of limitless possibility. It starts with recognising the origins of our thoughts—understanding that while we may inherit negative self-talk, we are also equipped with the ability to redefine that dialogue and emerge as allies in our own narratives. The journey is complex, but it begins within.

Rewriting the Script

Negative self-talk can often feel like an unrelenting echo in the chambers of our minds, resonating messages of inadequacy and doubt that chip away at our self-esteem and potential. However, the journey of overcoming this internal critic begins with a conscious decision to rewrite the script of our inner narratives. In this transformative process, we can become our own guardians, lifting ourselves from the depths of negativity into the light of self-empowerment.

To begin rewriting our internal script, we must first cultivate awareness. Awareness is the key that unlocks the door to change. When we become mindful of our thoughts, particularly those that are self-critical, we can start to identify patterns and triggers. Take a moment each day to observe these negative thoughts without judgment. Keep a thought journal, writing down instances of negative self-talk as they occur. This practice can help desensitise us to the negativity by bringing it into the light, allowing us to examine each thought critically.

For example, when you catch yourself thinking, "I always mess things up," challenge that statement. Ask yourself if it's really true. How many times have you succeeded? What about instances when you faced challenges but still prevailed? By dissecting these thoughts, we start to see them for what they are: distortions of reality rooted in fear and habit rather than truth.

Once we have identified our negative self-talk, the next step is reframing those thoughts into positive affirmations. Reframing is a powerful cognitive tool that enables us to shift our perspective from a negative to a positive one. When you notice a negative thought, consciously flip it into a positive one. Instead of "I'm not good enough," try "I am capable and worthy of success." Write down these reframed thoughts and repeat them daily. The more we affirm these positive statements, the more they begin to resonate within us, creating a new internal dialogue that fosters confidence and self-love.

In addition to reframing thoughts, journaling can be an effective tool for transforming our inner dialogue. Create a dedicated space in your journal for positive affirmations and reflections. List qualities you admire about yourself, accomplishments that instil pride, and moments when you overcame adversity. Reflect on your journey, acknowledging your struggles while celebrating your resilience. Over time, this practice can cultivate a reservoir of positivity that serves as an anchor during challenging times.

Another technique to incorporate into this process is self-compassion. Understand that everyone experiences negative self-talk at some point; it is a universal challenge. Being kind to ourselves during moments of self-doubt can dramatically change our outlook. When you encounter a critical thought, pause and treat yourself as you would treat a friend facing similar challenges. Would you tell them they are a failure? Or would you remind them of their worth, their efforts, and their strengths? By extending that same kindness to ourselves, we can cultivate a more compassionate inner dialogue. Integrating mindfulness into our daily routine also helps combat negative self-talk. Mindfulness encourages us to focus on the present moment rather than spiralling into past failures or future anxieties. Practice mindfulness through meditation, deep breathing exercises, or simple grounding techniques, such as paying attention to your breath. When thoughts of self-doubt emerge, acknowledge them without attachment; recognise them as fleeting and not a reflection of your true self. This practice will gradually help you detach from the weight of critical inner dialogues.

Further, creating a "supportive mantra" can serve as a powerful tool in rewriting our internal script. Choose a phrase that resonates with you and speaks to your aspirations or self-worth. It might be "I am enough," "I embrace my potential," or "I celebrate my journey." Repeat this mantra during moments of self-doubt. Visualise its meaning as you say it, allowing it to permeate your thoughts and replace negativity with positivity. Another helpful exercise is the "Positive Letter to Self." Write a letter addressed to yourself, detailing all the things you love about who you are. Reflect on your strengths, your achievements, and the things that make you unique. Make it a point to acknowledge not just successes but also the qualities that contribute to your character, such as your empathy, creativity, or determination. Revisit this letter when you need a reminder of your worth—it can serve as a tangible anchor in moments of self-doubt.

Engaging in regular self-reflection is also paramount in this journey. Set aside time each week for introspection, assessing your progress and addressing negative self-talk. Acknowledge the old patterns that resurface, but also celebrate the moments of growth and progress. Reflect on how your new affirmations have shifted your thinking. What changes have you noticed in your mood, confidence, or interactions with others? This assessment will help you recognise the effectiveness of your efforts while reinforcing the positives you wish to cultivate.

We must also recognise the influence of our environment on our internal narratives. Surround yourself with positivity—people who lift you, stories that inspire you, and experiences that enrich

We Are Our Own Enemies

you. Sometimes, our inner critic is amplified by external voices, and cultivating a supportive community can help mitigate this influence. Engage in conversations that uplift and encourage healthy self-reflection rather than dwelling on negativity or comparison.

As we embark on this journey of rewriting our internal script, it's important to understand that this is not a linear process. There will be setbacks and challenging days when negative self-talk seems louder than our affirmations. It's crucial to approach this journey with patience and perseverance. Remember that growth takes time and that every step forward, no matter how small, is significant. Celebrate these victories as they come, recognising that each moment of self-kindness strengthens the foundation of your new internal dialogue.

Additionally, seeking support can be a valuable component of this transformation. Consider discussing your journey with a trusted friend, mentor, or therapist. External perspectives can provide insights and encouragement, and they may help illuminate blind spots or challenge toxic thoughts you're unable to recognise in yourself. Professional guidance can be particularly beneficial in addressing deeper-rooted issues and patterns of negative self-talk that require more than surface-level intervention.

In our pursuit to rewrite the script, let's not forget the power of gratitude. Practising gratitude shifts our focus from what we lack to what we possess. Every night, write down three things you are grateful for, including positive experiences or aspects of yourself. This simple act can foster a mindset of abundance, framing our self-talk in a context that celebrates rather than criticises.

As we make strides in transforming our internal narratives, it's essential to remember that this is a lifelong journey. Embrace the process and be gentle with yourself. We learn and evolve every day, and our self-talk should reflect this growth. Each positive affirmation and each moment of self-compassion contribute to a tapestry of resilience that defines who we are.

In conclusion, the task of rewriting the script of our lives starts within. By acknowledging our negative self-talk and actively choosing to shift it towards positivity and affirmation, we begin to build a more supportive internal dialogue. This journey requires tools like journaling, reframing thoughts, self-compassion, mindfulness, and gratitude—all vital components in transforming the inner critic into an empowering voice of encouragement. As we cultivate this new narrative, we will unlock our potential to thrive, enabling us to overcome not only the challenges of our internal struggles but also to emerge as the allies we've always needed within ourselves. Each step taken on this path of self-discovery and affirmation brings us closer to the person we aspire to be, fostering not just individual resilience but more profound connections with others along the way.

We Are Our Own Enemies

Envy, Jealousy, and Comparison

Dark Companions

There was a time in my life when I walked the crowded streets feeling perpetually out of place. Friends and family surrounded me, yet a sense of loneliness enveloped me like a fog. I smiled at the world and tried to engage in conversations, yet deep down, a silent battle raged within, one that took the shape of dark companions: envy, jealousy, and comparison. They were not just fleeting thoughts; they were shadows lurking in my mind, whispering lies that warped my perception of myself and the world around me.

I remember the first time envy reared its head. I was at a friend's birthday party, happy for him yet simultaneously crushed by a sense of inadequacy. He had just secured a job offer from a prestigious company, while I was still uncertain about my own career path. As I watched him beam with joy, my mind turned toxic. Instead of celebrating his success, my heart cried out in bitterness, "Why not me?" The moment was tainted by my internal dialogue, the joys of his achievement overshadowed by the gaping wound of my own perceived failures.

Envy began as a ripple, a small wave that I thought I could control. But over time, it swelled into a tidal wave, dragging me under and suffocating me in its depths. I felt an uninvited resentment growing within me, a feeling that would magnify itself through my thoughts and actions. My conversations became tinged with sarcasm when discussing the successes of others, a shield to mask my vulnerabilities. The irony is that these dark companions convinced me they were protecting my self-esteem when, in fact, they were eroding it.

We Are Our Own Enemies

As I navigated through life, jealousy joined the fray, adding its own insidious layer to the mix. While envy is often about feeling inferior in comparison to someone else's success, jealousy took on a different form—it was the fear of being replaced. I became guarded in my friendships, especially when someone else entered the circle who seemed more talented or charming. I'd see friends spending time with new acquaintances, and irrational thoughts would flood my mind about being less favoured or valued. In these moments, my insecurity spiralled out of control.

It wasn't just about envy of achievements; it extended to appearance and character. Social media exacerbated this feeling. With every scroll through my feed, I was subjected to an endless parade of curated lives and manufactured perfection. Influencers showcasing their glamorous lifestyles would appear blissfully happy, and suddenly that dark companion of comparison would rear its ugly head again. I caught myself staring at my reflection, suffocated by an overwhelming conviction that I simply wasn't enough. I would ask myself endlessly: "Why do they have it all figured out when I am still floundering?" I didn't realise that I was allowing these uninvited feelings to dictate my self-worth.

In that measure, I became tangled in a web of toxic relationships, not just with others but also with myself. Through enlightening introspection, I recognised that envy, jealousy, and comparison bred isolation. In an effort to save face, I began sabotaging connections. I didn't just distance myself from those I envied; I also pushed away friends who celebrated achievements, fearing their pride would highlight my failings. I constructed barriers, confining myself to a solitary existence under the guise of self-preservation. The irony lay in the fact that in trying to shield my heart, I only invited more loneliness—my dark companions growing fonder as I drifted.

We Are Our Own Enemies

Despite this self-imposed isolation, the greatest revelation came when I began to recognise these emotions as indicators of deeper issues. David, a mutual friend, once expressed frustration at a colleague's meteoric rise in their shared workplace. He vented about the unfairness of it all, and I listened, nodding along at first. But then a flicker of awareness sparked within me. Rather than taking on his bitterness, I asked him why it bothered him so deeply. This opened a discussion that unveiled underlying fears of inadequacy related to his own career. That moment was an epiphany for me—both for him and for myself. In navigating through our shared pain, we illuminated the reality that these emotions were often reflections of our insecurities rather than genuine concerns.

Reflecting on these experiences, I realised that understanding these dark companions didn't equate to welcoming them. Awareness became my ally, leading me to confront the narratives that served as the breeding ground for envy and jealousy. I began to ask myself pivotal questions: Why do I feel less valuable when someone else shines? What about their accomplishment threatens my self-concept? This self-inquiry sparked a shift. Instead of seeing others as adversaries, I experimented with viewing them as allies in a shared journey. Their success could exist independently of my worth; their victories didn't diminish mine.

Journeying inward revealed that comparison acted as a thief of joy, diverting my focus from self-improvement to an obsessive scrutiny of others. As I shifted my mindset, instead of ranking myself against peers, I focused on celebrating my unique journey. I began journaling daily, noting down personal milestones—large and small—and recognising my growth. This was an antidote to the corrosive influences of envy and comparison; self-reflection became a fertile ground to cultivate gratitude.

We Are Our Own Enemies

As I unearthed layers of self-compassion, jealousy gradually transformed into admiration. Upon meeting new successes, I'd catch myself asking, "What can I learn from them?" If their talents inspired me, might those talents push me toward my own goals? Celebrating others' achievements became a practice in gratitude instead of grievance. Transitioning from a zero-sum perspective to an abundance mindset—believing there was enough space for everyone to thrive—was a liberating discovery. I learned that another's success did not doom my journey but rather illuminated pathways I hadn't considered.

Yet self-reflection often requires help. In acknowledging my struggles, I sought mentorship, not just from those who had succeeded but also from those who candidly shared their setbacks. Each story became a lesson in resilience, a reminder of how envy and comparison are fruits of our humanity, rather than flaws to hide. These conversations became communal, breaking down the walls I previously believed I had to uphold.

Through ongoing dialogue, I learned that everyone wrestles with envy and comparison in some form. Vulnerability shattered the façades we held, reshaping relationships into strongholds of empathy. I witnessed friends embrace their imperfections, and those moments became treasures; they were not signs of weakness but bridges connecting our experiences. Together, we attempted to redefine success not as an isolated achievement but as a collective victory.

The implications of these deepening connections reverberated beyond individual relationships. In witnessing others untangle their insecurities, I started to notice how envy, jealousy, and comparison seep into our wider social fabric. These emotions form fertile ground for division. We undermine our collective unity by allowing dark influences to infiltrate our perceptions of one another. I pondered how much potential might go unrealised if we consider ourselves in perpetual competition. We lose sight of the significance of community—a place where shared experiences can elevate collective growth.

As the dynamics within my circle shifted, so did my understanding of the world at large. In confronting my dark companions, I unearthed layers of empathy within me that extended beyond my personal confines. I began to see stories instead of accolades—stories of sleepless nights and struggles, of perseverance and grit wrapped up in different packages. I witnessed grand achievements in light of the sacrifices and hard work behind them. This cultivated a rich tapestry of human experience, one in which I no longer saw individuals through the lens of adequacy, but rather as unique threads contributing to a shared story of resilience.

Through my journey, I began to understand that these dark companions thrive on isolation. They feed off silence and secrecy, growing more potent in an environment devoid of light. When we find the courage to speak about them, we strip them of their power. We create a collective narrative that embraces humanity's complexities—the shared struggles, triumphs, and, yes, moments of envy too. By sharing stories, we create a community that can hold space for vulnerability without judgment.

In this understanding, I have grown to wield my experience with dark companions as a catalyst for transformation. The emotions that once confined me now serve as markers, guiding me towards greater self-awareness and connection. Rather than allowing envy, jealousy, and comparison to dictate my self-worth, I have embraced them as tools for growth, recognising that genuine happiness doesn't stem from achieving someone else's benchmarks but rather in aligning with my values and passions.

As this chapter of my life unfolds, I invite you to explore the intricate dynamics of these emotions as well. Envy, jealousy, and comparison—consider them as remnants of self-preservation that, when acknowledged, can serve as mirrors reflecting our desires for growth. Embrace vulnerability in discussing these feelings openly; it is through this exploration that we will combat the negativity they breed. Let us transform dark companions into motivators on our paths toward fulfilment and connection, celebrating our victories while lifting each other higher in our collective journeys of becoming.

Cultivating Gratitude

Gratitude is often described as a feeling of appreciation and thankfulness. However, it is much more than that; it's an active practice that can shift our perception of life and inherently counteract the destructive emotions of envy, jealousy, and comparison. As we explore ways to cultivate gratitude, we will uncover how this simple yet profound practice can serve as a remedy in navigating the choppy waters of our emotions, redirecting our energies from what we lack to what we possess.

Understanding the sense of want that arises from envy requires an introspective examination of what we allow to influence our thoughts and feelings. Throughout our lives, we're constantly bombarded by images, narratives, and experiences that highlight what others have achieved or acquired. Social media platforms have amplified this effect, creating a culture of comparison where we often view the curated lives of others through rose-coloured glasses, overlooking the struggles, disappointments, and heartaches that may exist beneath the surface.

We Are Our Own Enemies

Gratitude offers a path back to contentment, serving as a reminder that while we may be aware of what others have, we also possess the power to appreciate our own circumstances, achievements, and life's simple joys. As we practice gratitude, we build resilience against envy and jealousy, reframing our mindsets from a position of lack to one of abundance, thereby nurturing a culture of contentment within ourselves.

One practical way to cultivate gratitude is through journaling. Set aside a few moments each day or week to reflect on what you're thankful for, no matter how small it may seem. Start with the basics: a warm cup of coffee in the morning, the laughter shared with a friend, the beauty of a sunset, or the comfort of a well-worn chair. By focusing on these positive aspects, you can create a foundation for your gratitude practice.

Consider a prompt to guide your reflection: "Write about three instances today when you felt grateful." Allow yourself to explore the feelings associated with those moments. What emotions did they evoke? How did they affect your day? By actively identifying and acknowledging these moments, you reinforce the neural pathways that calibrate your mind toward appreciation rather than envy.

Similarly, stories and anecdotes provide powerful illustrations of transformation through gratitude. Reflect on a client, Sarah, whom I had the pleasure of coaching. Sarah was perpetually discontent, plagued by feelings of comparison. She often envied her colleagues who seemed to be advancing in their careers while she felt stuck. During our sessions, we introduced her to a gratitude jar—an idea that transformed her perspective. Each evening, Sarah would write down something positive that had happened that day on a small piece of paper and place it in the jar. Over time, she realised that the moments of joy in her life were far more abundant than she had ever acknowledged.

A key aspect of cultivating gratitude lies in its simplicity. We can begin with small acts of reflection and gradually build them into daily rituals. You might try the practice of "grateful mornings," where, upon waking, you take a few minutes to mentally list what you are thankful for before rising from bed. This sets a positive tone for the day ahead.

Another approach is to practice gratitude before meals, taking a moment to recognise the effort that went into preparing the food, the nourishment it provides, and the company you share it with. These small practices ground you in the present moment and remind you of the beauty that exists in the everyday experience.

Alongside these routines, regular moments of mindfulness can further enhance your capacity for gratitude. By being present and fully engaged in each moment, you will become more attuned to the gifts of life as they unfold around you. Consider a simple breathing exercise: close your eyes, focus on your breath, and with each inhalation, think of something you appreciate. With each exhalation, release negative thoughts tied to envy and jealousy. This small act encourages a mental shift, promoting a sense of calmness and gratitude.

In nurturing an attitude of gratitude, we might also consider the impact of community and relationships. Expressing gratitude toward others not only strengthens bonds but also builds a positive feedback loop. When we acknowledge the contributions of others, whether through a simple thank-you note or verbal acknowledgement, we create an environment where gratitude flourishes. A coaching client, Michael, dedicated a week to writing personal notes of appreciation to colleagues and family members.

The ripple effect was profound; not only did he experience contentment from sharing gratitude, but he also witnessed a shift in the way those around him interacted.

Gratitude can also be cultivated by recognising the struggles we endure. Sometimes, difficult circumstances serve as powerful lessons, leading us to a place of deeper appreciation. For instance, reflecting on a challenging experience might reveal strengths you were previously unaware of or insights that become sources of gratitude. As we apply this lens, we invite a reflective practice that doesn't shy away from adversity but instead recognises it as an integral part of our growth.

As we delve deeper into gratitude as a practice, we must also confront the cultural narratives that encourage comparison and jealousy. The drive to appear successful often leads us to portray ourselves in a light that may not entirely reflect our truths, causing cycles of envy. Mindfully challenging these norms can free us from anxieties about underachieving. Embracing the belief that each individual's journey is unique allows us to cultivate our energy toward self-compassion rather than harmful comparison.

Engaging with gratitude can also take the form of creative expression. Consider channels such as art, music, or writing as outlets for expressing appreciation. Writing poetry inspired by moments of gratitude or composing a song that honours the people who've made a difference in your life can deepen the connection to what you're thankful for. These creative practices can enrich our ability to recognise and articulate gratitude, solidifying its place in our lives.

In addition to journaling and creative expressions, developing a gratitude practice can be enhanced through discussion. Engaging in conversations about what you are grateful for, whether in group settings, with friends, or even in therapy sessions, helps to reaffirm insight and strengthen connections. It becomes a shared exploration of appreciation that can positively influence those around you. When we openly acknowledge the good in our lives, we cultivate a culture that values gratitude, thereby counteracting the toxicity of envy and jealousy.

Thoughtfully incorporating gratitude into your social interactions can not only shift your individual experience but also the collective atmosphere around you. Be it in family gatherings, friendships, or community groups, openly sharing gratitude can inspire others to reflect on and cultivate their own appreciation. This cycle of gratitude fosters deeper relationships and strengthens community ties, benefiting everyone involved.

To truly integrate gratitude into your life, consider weaving it into the fabric of your daily routines. Create rituals that celebrate what you value. Perhaps express your gratitude at the start of meetings, take a moment at the end of each day to reflect on what went well, or develop family traditions focused on appreciation, such as sharing what each member is thankful for during special gatherings. These daily practices not only enhance our moral frameworks but also anchor us in moments of thankfulness, transforming our perceptions.

As we journey further into the practice of gratitude, we can explore the role of mindfulness and meditation. These techniques foster a deeper connection to the present moment, enabling us to fully appreciate the beauty of our surroundings and experiences. By meditating on gratitude, we cultivate an intricate web of awareness that highlights what we have, rather than what we lack.

We Are Our Own Enemies

Consider dedicating a portion of your meditation time to gratitude: focus on the people who have supported you, the lessons learned along the way, or the simple beauty found in nature's presence. Allow the feelings of appreciation to guide your breath, expanding the mindset of abundance within you.

To create lasting change through gratitude, reflect on the intentions behind your practice. These intentions can act as guiding principles to foster a deeper connection to all life offers. Challenge yourself to define what gratitude means to you personally and how you can bring that vision to life in your daily actions. This can be a deeply transformational exercise, as it roots your practice in your unique expectations and values.

As you cultivate this spirit of gratitude, creating a support system can reinforce your journey. Surround yourself with individuals who share the same values and can help hold you accountable. Encourage one another to engage in regular discussions about gratitude and its impact on your lives. By forming connections based on gratitude, you dilute the potency of envy and jealousy, ultimately enriching the bonds you share with others.

Remember, cultivating gratitude takes time and persistence. It may feel foreign at first, especially if you are accustomed to a focus on competition and comparison. However, as you remain committed to this practice, you will gradually notice a shift in your mindset. Life's challenges may not disappear, but your reactions to them and your perceptions of self-worth and success will evolve.

In the long run, the practice of gratitude is about shifting from "Why them?" to "Thank goodness I have." When we adopt this perspective, we redefine success by creating a lens through which joy and appreciation radiate abundantly into our lives, regardless of external circumstances or achievements.

As you embark on this journey to cultivate gratitude, acknowledge and embrace the moments when envy or comparison arise. Instead of pushing them away, acknowledge them. Then gently return your focus to your own experiences, inviting appreciation into your heart. By doing so, you transform these feelings from enemies into guides leading you back toward self-acceptance and contentment.

In conclusion, integrating gratitude into our lives serves as a powerful means of escaping the shadows of envy, jealousy, and comparison. Through dedicated practices like journaling, mindfulness, and relationship building, we can shift our focus from what we lack to the wealth of experiences and connections that enrich our lives. By embracing and nurturing gratitude, we cultivate a culture of contentment within ourselves, enabling us to navigate life's complexities with greater ease and appreciation. In doing so, we take significant steps toward becoming our own allies, transforming our inner landscape into one filled with light, abundance, and joy.

Building Compassionate Connections

In a world where social media casts a vast spotlight on others' lives, feelings of envy and jealousy can creep in, seemingly uninvited. It has become all too easy to scroll through carefully curated images and snippets of others' lives and feel our self-worth diminish in their shadow. But what if instead of succumbing to these negative feelings, we chose to build compassionate connections with those around us? By opting for community over comparison, we can enrich our lives and transform the very nature of our interactions.

Consider the story of two friends, Emma and Mia, who grew up in the same neighbourhood and attended the same school. Despite their shared experiences, each followed a different path post-

We Are Our Own Enemies

graduation. Emma quickly climbed the corporate ladder, landing a coveted role at an esteemed marketing firm. Mia, on the other hand, found herself navigating a more winding path, jumping between jobs and unsure of her career trajectory. Social media became a battleground for their perspectives; every new promotion Emma posted felt like a reminder of Mia's uncertainties. Envy began to erode their friendship, creating an invisible wall fuelled by comparison.

The turning point came when Emma noticed it. Sitting alone in her apartment, she felt an unexpected wave of guilt wash over her as she scrolled through Mia's social feed—a highlight reel of celebrations, supportive comments, and reminders of how vibrant friendship could be. Instead of feeling excited for her friend, she felt a heaviness in her heart. That night, for the first time, she found the courage to reach out to Mia: "Hey, I've been meaning to check in. Let's grab coffee this week."

When they met, Emma expressed her gratitude for Mia's unwavering support through tough times. They laughed, reminisced, and, finally, strayed away from past comparisons. Mia admitted that instead of feeling happy for Emma, she often felt resentful and lost. That candid conversation shifted their dynamic. They replaced envy with empathy. They agreed to celebrate each other's successes, allowing vulnerability and compassion to flourish, thus dismantling the barriers their previous envy had erected.

This experience illustrates the first crucial aspect of building compassionate connections: prioritising authentic communication. Discussion lays the groundwork upon which mutual understanding is built. Many times, we harbour assumptions about others' experiences without truly understanding the depth or complexity of their journeys. By sharing honestly about our highs and lows, we open doors to deeper relationships that thrive on empathy instead of competition. Emma and Mia's candid conversation revealed the common ground they shared: the struggle to find their place in the world.

Furthermore, cultivating an environment where support thrives fosters positive and uplifting relationship dynamics. Embracing vulnerability, which can often feel intimidating, enables connections that allow individuals to feel seen and validated in their emotions. This act is foundational to shifting the narrative from one of comparison to one of community. When we share our fears, failures, and triumphs, we find that many experiences are universal, thus easing the burdens of isolation and promoting shared healing.

Consider the example of a community garden, a simple yet profound metaphor. In this garden, no two plants are the same, yet each plays a unique role in the ecosystem. Just as plants require interdependence to flourish—shading one another, competing for sunlight, and sharing nutrients—our relationships can thrive in interconnectedness, forming resilient bonds that overshadow feelings of envy. Every plant strives toward its own flourish, leading to a beautiful, diverse garden, much like a community that celebrates the uniqueness of its members while fostering collaborative growth. The more we extend ourselves to those around us, the more we cultivate a space that encourages communal flourishing rather than places of competition.

In fostering community, we also need to reflect upon how we approach achievement and success. The paradigm of individual accomplishment easily leads us into the trap of comparison. However, when we recognise that every success can simultaneously contribute to the success of others, we pave the way for collaborative journeys. For instance, in a company's work environment, one employee's success at leading a project doesn't diminish another's value. Rather, it can provide an avenue for mentorship, collaboration, and shared learning experiences. About a year ago, a small creative agency invited its team members to begin a 'success board' in their common area. Employees could write down their achievements—big or small—on sticky notes and pin them to the board. When one person achieved a goal, the entire team celebrated it, creating an atmosphere of support and collective pride. Instead of cultivating envy, it shifted their focus to shared success, showcasing how interconnected efforts created a thriving community.

Empathetic relationships also mean recognising when we have fallen victim to the comparison mindset and choosing to take action against it. For example, Sarah found herself in a cycle of jealousy when her friend Lisa posted about landing her dream job. Instead of expressing her excitement for Lisa, Sarah began to quietly resent her friend and withdrew from their relationship. However, an opportunity arose when they attended a mutual friend's birthday party. In one of their conversations, Sarah finally shared her feelings. To her surprise, Lisa responded with understanding, revealing that she, too, had experienced moments of self-doubt and feelings of inadequacy. This heart-to-heart moment marked the start of a new chapter in their friendship. By voicing her discomfort instead of letting it fester, Sarah reclaimed the connection by understanding that Lisa had not only earned her success but also faced her own challenges. This exchange strengthened their friendship, showing how empathy can flourish when we approach relationships with honesty and relatability. A significant aspect of dismantling jealousy and envy is also understanding the underlying motivations of these feelings. Often, what lies at the core of comparison becomes a reflection of our own insecurities. When we experience envy toward someone else's accomplishments, it highlights our desires and aspirations. Instead of allowing it to breed bitterness, we can actively choose to direct that energy toward personal growth. By reframing our responses to envy as an indicator of what we wish to cultivate within ourselves, we can shift from a mindset of comparison to one of inspiration.

For instance, Alex felt envious of his colleague Jennifer, who consistently received accolades and positive feedback. Instead of sulking in his feelings, Alex took it upon himself to learn from Jennifer's work ethic. He approached her, expressing admiration for her abilities and interest in developing his professional skills. Jennifer was delighted and offered to share strategies that had been beneficial for her. This marked the beginning of a mentorship bond that not only advanced Alex's career but also deepened friendships among coworkers. It's a vivid example of how embracing collaboration over crippling envy can lead to collective advancement.

Additionally, a vibrant community thrives on inclusive celebrations. By making an intentional effort to celebrate each other's successes, we foster a culture that reinforces compassion. We can organise gatherings, share milestones, and utilise social platforms to amplify each other's achievements. Community initiatives that encourage shared victories can amplify feelings of belonging, reinforcing a sense of togetherness rather than isolation.

Incorporating rituals that honour achievements is vital. For example, consider a workplace that holds monthly meetings to highlight individual or team achievements. These celebrations could include sharing personal growth stories or recognising contributions that may otherwise go unnoticed. By establishing these rituals, we signal to one another that the journey is just as important as the successes it yields. Reinforcing the importance of community during times of triumph helps diminish the urge to compare ourselves with one another.

Moreover, nurturing compassion means addressing and supporting those who are struggling. We must cultivate spaces where vulnerability is welcomed and encouraged. A friend recently shared her struggles with burnout at work, and instead of offering quick solutions or dismissing her feelings, I made a conscious effort to listen actively and create a safe space for her to be heard. We discussed her feelings for an extended period, exploring ways to prioritise wellness together. This act of sharing and supporting not only brought us closer together but also helped alleviate the stress of my own insecurities.

In essence, building compassionate connections involves a continual commitment to supporting one another without judgment. It requires a conscious effort to replace transactional relationships with deeper bonds that are rooted in empathy, kindness, and mutual respect. When we prioritise connections over comparisons, we craft an environment where compassion flourishes among friends, families, and communities—resulting in a rich tapestry of interconnected lives.

As we move forward, let us challenge our instincts that veer toward envy and comparison. Instead, let's cultivate an appreciation for the unique paths each person walks. By consciously choosing to engage with others in meaningful ways, we remind ourselves that humanity is inherently interconnected. Just as roots intertwine beneath the surface of a thriving forest, our own connections provide nourishment and sustenance in times of hardship as well as rejoicing.

These compassionate connections cultivate an environment in which we all feel valued and understood. Envy and jealousy dissolve when we choose kindness, empathy, and support. Reach out to those in your sphere, replace envy with gratitude, and remind yourself that every human story holds beauty, complexity, and interconnectedness.

In conclusion, to genuinely replace comparisons with community-building requires vulnerability, shared narratives, and a commitment to celebrating one another. It involves recognising that the journey is not a solo expedition, but a collective experience. Each of us has the power to craft a space of compassionate connections that enriches our lives and helps dismantle feelings of envy and jealousy. By investing in our relationships with empathy, we not only create a supportive tapestry for ourselves but also pave the way for future generations to flourish within interconnected communities. Indeed, the most powerful antidote to the envy that plagues our hearts is found in the bonds we forge with one another. Let us endeavour to nurture these connections, transforming our realities from solitary struggles into shared victories.

We Are Our Own Enemies

The Fear of Success

Success Paradox

Success is often heralded as the ultimate achievement—the culmination of hard work, dedication, and vision. Yet, paradoxically, it is also a source of deep-seated fear for many. As we embark on the journey toward realising our dreams and aspirations, just before the finish line, a peculiar phenomenon takes shape. It is in these crucial moments of potential breakthrough that internal conflicts bubble to the surface—a swirling tempest of doubt, anxiety, and trepidation. The exploration of this paradox—an aversion to what is typically seen as the pinnacle of fulfilment—deserves our scrutiny.

Let us first unpack the essence of success. To many, success embodies personal, professional, and financial achievements. It signifies the pinnacle of social standing, the accumulation of wealth, and the acknowledgement of our efforts and dreams. It is viewed as validation of one's worth and capabilities —a legacy that one can pass on to future generations. The notion of success is often enshrined in our culture, glorified in stories of triumph, and underscored by countless motivational quotes that implore us to chase our dreams relentlessly. How, then, can the very idea of success trigger apprehension?

The Seeker, that voice within each of us yearning for purpose and fulfilment, often wrestles with the weight of expectation. When we approach the precipice of our goals—the tangible achievement of what we have long desired—our internal landscape can shift dramatically. Suddenly, moments that were once filled with excitement and anticipation become overshadowed by questions of identity, worthiness, and fear of the unknown. Thanks to an array of psychological factors, insight into this unsettling paradox reveals the intricacies governing our relationship with success.

First and foremost, among these factors is the fear of change. For many, achieving success propels an individual into unfamiliar territory. With success comes a new reality, often accompanied by expectations and responsibilities that can be daunting to accept. The concept of the "unknown" weighs heavily on the human psyche, prompting feelings of vulnerability. We often become comfortable with the status quo, even if it is riddled with discontent. Success calls for adaptation, and for some, the prospect of change can feel more threatening than enduring the familiar discomfort of a less-than-satisfactory existence.

This leads us to another underlying cause of our trepidation: impostor syndrome. This psychological pattern finds fertile ground among high achievers who struggle with chronic self-doubt, fostering encapsulating fears of being "found out" as a fraud. As successes accumulate, so too does the fear that one's achievements are merely results of luck or favourable circumstances. When faced with higher stakes, this internal critic can amplify, convincing the Seeker that full recognition of their talents and abilities will inevitably lead to failure—a fear so potent it can lead one to sabotage their own chances at success.

Moreover, the fear of success intertwines with our innate human need for belonging and acceptance. Achieving success may inadvertently alienate us from our peers, instilling a fear of changing societal dynamics. Relationships can shift drastically when achievements lead to disparities in status, wealth, or power. In a society that often embraces mediocrity while chastising triumph, those on the brink of success might wrestle with the fear of ostracisation. The Seeker may question: "Will I still be accepted if I outshine my friends or family?" Such internalised communal apprehension can drive one to self-sabotage as a misguided effort to maintain social harmony.

As we delve deeper into the psychological underpinnings of this paradox, we encounter the role of perfectionism in the landscape of fear surrounding success. The quest for excellence can morph into an unattainable goal, leading individuals to believe they must meet exacting standards to achieve success. The conscious and subconscious pressure to produce flawless results can prevent many from reaching for the opportunities that lie just at their fingertips. The pursuit of the perfect moment to act can morph into an insidious cycle of procrastination, where fear of inadequacy stifles initiative. The Seeker becomes ensnared in a web spun from high expectations, which often culminates in avoidance of the very success they crave.

What compounds the success paradox further is our social conditioning. We are often bombarded with narratives about success—the stories of those who rise, only to fall, and the relentless grind required to achieve status. As observers of such narratives, we internalise cautionary tales that reinforce apprehension. The looming possibility of failure exists in stark contrast to the celebration of success, and these stories can seep into our psyche, creating an unshakeable fear of stepping into the limelight. The Seeker thus faces an internal struggle between ambition and fear, with cultural narratives serving as both inspiration and threat.

As we explore the experiences surrounding success, it is critical to consider the role of self-worth. Many individuals tie their identity and sense of value to their accomplishments. In doing so, success becomes not merely a benchmark but a reflection of one's worthiness. When framed in this light, the fear of success is rooted in the possibility of revealing oneself as insufficient if achievements fall short of expectations. The pressure to continually validate one's self-image through accomplishments fosters a cycle of anxiety and dread. Suddenly, the pinnacle of success transforms into a high-stakes game with everything on the line, and the stakes of failure feel intolerable.

The moments leading up to pivotal success often become fraught with anticipation, balancing precariously between hope and fear. As we stand on the brink, the Seeker must navigate the turbulent waters of inner conflict. Recognising this paradox is essential in the journey toward self-awareness and growth. Understanding the roots of this fear equips us to confront the internal battles and navigate the complexities of success and aspirations.

Reflecting on the narrative of fear and success, it is imperative to address the societal pressures and expectations that amplify this internal struggle. Professional trajectories often come laced with the expectation of rapid success—a metric measured against peers, industry benchmarks, and personal goals. In such an environment, it is understandable that many succumb to fear rather than embracing the potential for success. The Seeker is caught in a race against time, where the fear of falling behind or of not "making it" can paralyse even the most driven individuals. The lingering notion that success is a finite resource—that if someone else possesses it, it diminishes the chances for others—creates an adversarial relationship with aspirations.

Moreover, societal structures often perpetuate the narrative of scarcity, which contrasts with the abundance mindset. The fear of success breeds an underlying notion that achievements come at a cost. In workplaces, contexts of competition and comparison can lead to adversarial relationships between colleagues. The pursuit of success thus becomes a battlefield, where individuals grapple with

We Are Our Own Enemies

anxiety and insecurity rather than camaraderie and shared achievements. This hostile environment stifles collaboration, further undermining the potential for the collective success of teams and communities.

In summary, the fear of success represents a complex tapestry woven from psychological distress, societal pressures, and deeply ingrained beliefs about identity and worth. It forces the Seeker to navigate a landscape rife with conflict where ambition is often countered by self-doubt, anxiety, and cultural narratives. The recognition of this paradox gives voice to the internal struggles that arise just before we are poised to cross the threshold into achieving our aspirations.

Through the lens of psychotherapy, self-development, and introspective practices, we can unravel these fears and forge a path toward embracing success without the shackles of self-sabotage. Acknowledging the fear serves as the first step in disarming it, creating space for dialogue about our ambitions and aspirations. By delving into our motivations and the narratives we tell ourselves, we can shift our perspective to view success not merely as an endpoint, but as an evolving journey—one that encompasses not only our achievements but also our growth as individuals.

Ultimately, what is required is an honest confrontation with the very fears that seek to derail our paths. This means understanding that fear, while potent, can be transformed into a source of awareness and insight. By reframing our perceptions, we can cultivate a healthier relationship with success, replacing fear with curiosity and excitement about the possibilities that lie ahead. By changing the narrative around success, from one of mere achievement to a celebration of individual growth, we anchor ourselves in resilience rather than apprehension.

As we delve into the intricacies of the success paradox, we recognise that it is an integral part of our human experience. The Seeker within us yearns for fulfilment, and with deliberate self-reflection and understanding, we can step past the fear and embrace the beautiful complexities of what it means to succeed. The journey may be filled with uncertainty, but it also holds boundless potential—a journey worthy of pursuing despite the trepidation. In doing so, we transform not just our relationship with success but also our inner dialogues, ultimately becoming allies in our quest for growth, purpose, and meaningful accomplishments.

Redefining Success

Success is a concept often shrouded in societal ideals that dictate its very meaning. It is frequently associated with wealth, achievement, prestige, and visibility; characteristics that provide a comfortable narrative for what one might aspire to be. However, these external markers of success can often cloud our understanding of what it truly means to thrive in life. In this section, we will delve into the concept of redefining success. We aim to challenge the external frameworks that dictate our aspirations and instead encourage a more nuanced view that reflects our individual values and aspirations.

In our journey to understand success, it is essential to first recognise the factors that shape our definitions. Society is a powerful teacher, shaping our notions of success from an early age. As children, we are inundated with messages—through media, educational systems, and our families—about what makes someone 'successful.' High grades, prestigious schools, lucrative jobs, and public acknowledgement are often hailed as the ultimate achievements. These ideals create a blueprint that many feel pressured to follow, leading to a relentless pursuit of accomplishments that may not fully resonate with their true selves.

We Are Our Own Enemies

Moreover, this conventional perspective can engender a fear of success. For some, the societal pressure to attain visible markers of success becomes a double-edged sword. They may find themselves driven to reach these heights, yet, in the back of their minds, the question looms—what if I achieve this and still feel unfulfilled? This fear of discovering that traditional success doesn't equate to personal happiness can be paralysing and prevent many from even attempting to pursue their dreams.

To redefine success, we must first identify our inherent values. What truly matters to us? Is it health, happiness, creativity, connection, or perhaps something entirely different? Reflecting upon personal values is a critical first step in cultivating an authentic vision of success. This is often an introspective journey, requiring us to step away from societal influences and examine our beliefs, desires, and what brings us genuine joy. Engaging in self-reflection can involve various methods, from journaling to deep contemplative practices. The key is to ask ourselves probing questions: What moments have brought me joy? What contributions to the world do I find most fulfilling? How do I wish to be remembered? As we engage with these inquiries, we can begin to shape a more personalised definition of success—one that resonates with our unique life experiences and ambitions.

Once we have an understanding of our values, it becomes essential to distil these insights into an authentic vision of success. This process may involve envisioning what a 'successful' life looks like, specifically for us. Instead of visualising a high-powered job or a lavish lifestyle, we might picture nurturing relationships, a balanced work-life ethos, or contributing to causes close to our hearts. This vision should be fuelled by passion rather than external validation—imagine chasing interests without the interference of comparison or fear.

We Are Our Own Enemies

In examining alternative definitions of success, we can draw inspiration from figures who have disrupted the traditional narrative. Many influential leaders, artists, and thinkers have advocated for the idea that true success stems from living authentically and making meaningful contributions. For instance, rather than accumulating wealth, the philanthropic efforts of individuals like Oprah Winfrey reflect how giving back can be a profound marker of success. When we align our lives with our values and passions, we often find that fulfilment follows, often in unexpected and enriching ways.

As we redefine success, let us also consider the concept of potential. Fear can often lead us to shrink back from pursuing what we are truly capable of. It might whisper that our dreams are too ambitious or that we are unworthy of achieving greatness. Yet, embracing our potential requires us to confront these fears head-on. What if, instead of shying away from ambition, we regarded it as a calling? Understanding that we have the capacity for greatness can inspire us to take action. It requires us to clarify our goals and, more significantly, recognise that potential includes the journey and growth involved in pursuing those goals. This shift in perspective enables us to perceive setbacks not as failures, but as integral parts of our development—a necessary step in honing our skills and nurturing resilience.

With a new perspective on success and an embrace of our potential, we can actively pursue our redefined vision. Setting ambitious yet attainable goals aligns with the authentic vision we tailored earlier. Goals should be reflections of our values and passions rather than society's mould. Establishing this connection enables us to pursue these aims with enthusiasm rather than fear, infusing joy into the process that can easily be lost in its pursuit.

We Are Our Own Enemies

Yet, the path to success is rarely a linear one. Embracing this complexity is crucial in our journey. There will be challenges, obstacles, and the occasional questioning of our path. It's important to remind ourselves that setbacks do not define us; they often refine us. In these moments, ensuring we maintain a support system—be it friends, mentors, or community—can help us navigate doubt and remind us of our potential.

As we redefine success, let's also acknowledge the importance of celebrating small victories. These milestones reinforce our commitment to our authentic vision, allowing us to appreciate the journey. Each step forward, whether big or small, should be recognised, for they collectively contribute to our overall growth and fulfilment. Ultimately, redefining success is an ongoing process that intertwines self-awareness, values, potential, and perseverance. It transcends mere achievements as it cultivates an understanding of what it truly means to thrive in our own unique way. The narrative that our lives must adhere to conventional standards can be rewritten, and doing so can liberate us from the fear of inadequacy.

To further illustrate the concept, consider the metaphor of a tree. A tree's success can be viewed through its height, the number of flowers it produces, or the size of its trunk. However, a tree's true success lies within its roots, the depth and strength that allow it to withstand storms and grow steadily over time. Similarly, the strength of our own definition of success should not be superficially measured by external circumstances, but rather be rooted deeply in our values and personal growth. Let us redefine success as a journey—a roadmap that navigates towards personal fulfilment, authenticity, and impact. We must remember that our story is uniquely ours to write, filled with the colours of our aspirations and the hues of our experiences. Embracing this narrative as one of possibility rather than fear opens doors to fulfilling lives where success is not just an attainment but an embodiment of who we authentically are.

In conclusion, redefining success can become a transformative practice, lighting the path towards acting in alignment with our true selves. The journey encourages us to look beyond the surface, to reflect deeply on our values, and to embrace our full potential without the intimidation of traditional expectations. It is when we strip away these layers of societal pressure that we can finally see ourselves for who we truly are—the architects of our dreams and the authors of our destined success stories. As we step into this new realm, we unlock not only our own potential but also the possibility for others to do the same, collectively shaping a world where success is as diverse and dynamic as the individuals who pursue it.

Embracing Risks

In the journey towards achieving our dreams, the fear of success often looms larger than the fear of failure. It serves as an invisible barrier, imprisoning our potential and stifling our aspirations. This fear, deeply rooted in our experiences, societal expectations, and internal narratives, can paralyse our ambitions and shackle our creativity. Yet, true success is inherently entwined with risk. To step beyond the confines of our fears and embrace the possibility of greatness, we must make a deliberate choice to confront and transcend our apprehension. To navigate the treacherous waters of risk-taking, we need to equip ourselves with strategies that empower us to leap fearlessly into pursuing our dreams. This final subchapter presents actionable steps to embrace risks and invites you to recognise your worthiness of joy and achievement. It is about transforming the daunting burden of fear into a source of strength. This transformation begins with understanding the nature of risk itself. Recognising the Value of Risks. At the core of embracing risk is the realisation that it is not merely a step into the unknown, but an opportunity for extraordinary growth. Every successful person you admire has faced risks along their journey—what separates them from those who remain stagnant is their capacity to embrace uncertainty rather than avoid it. They recognise that progress seldom occurs in environments of certainty; rather, it blooms in the soil of risk, vulnerability, and brave exploration.

Begin by re-evaluating your relationship with risk. Instead of perceiving it solely as a potential for loss, shift your mindset to view risk as an essential ingredient in the recipe for success. It can be advantageous to define what risk means to you. Is it the chance of failure? The fear of judgment from others? The discomfort of change? Acknowledging these factors will enable you to confront them head-on. Take a moment to reflect on past experiences where you took risks—no matter how small—and assess the results. What did you learn? How did you grow? Often, the most daunting risks lead to the most profound lessons. Use these reflections to cultivate a narrative of resilience that emphasises the positive outcomes of risk-taking, even amidst failures.

Shifting Your Mindset. Mindset is the lens through which we interpret our world. Cultivating a growth mindset, as defined by psychologist Carol Dweck, enables us to view challenges as opportunities for learning rather than obstacles. This fundamental shift is transformative, enabling us to celebrate effort, perseverance, and learning over mere outcomes. Implement strategies to reinforce a growth mindset. Practice self-compassion by acknowledging your fears without judgment. Understand that fear is a natural human emotion; it does not diminish your worth or your potential. Affirmation exercises can help build your confidence by regularly reminding yourself of your abilities, successes, and unique strengths. Document your achievements, no matter how small, and revisit them when you encounter self-doubt.

Additionally, surround yourself with a supportive community that encourages risk-taking. Engage with individuals who inspire you to pursue your dreams, who celebrate your victories, and who offer constructive feedback. The energy of progressive thinking is contagious; often, the people we associate with significantly influence our mindset. Setting Clear Intentions. Before leaping, it is crucial to clarify your intentions. Identify what success looks like for you personally. In the midst of our busy lives, we often drift along, reacting to circumstances rather than actively crafting our destinies. By setting clear intentions, you establish a roadmap that guides your actions towards your aspirations.

Begin with a vision board that visually represents your goals, dreams, and what success means to you. Allow this exercise to ignite your imagination and enthusiasm. This tangible representation serves as a constant reminder of your larger purpose, providing motivation during moments of doubt.

Alongside visual tools, articulate your intentions in writing. Practice the technique of journaling, where you chronicle your thoughts, aspirations, and fears. By externalising your internal dialogue, you clarify your desires and reinforce your commitment to pursuing them. This practice fosters accountability, encouraging you to take progressive steps.

Embracing Discomfort. It is crucial to accept that discomfort is an integral part of growth. The path toward success is rarely smooth; the most significant transformations often occur when we stretch beyond our comfort zones. Embracing discomfort involves cultivating a tolerance for uncertainty, leaning into the unknown with curiosity rather than trepidation.

We Are Our Own Enemies

Consider undertaking small challenges that provoke a sense of discomfort. Public speaking, networking, or trying out a new skill can serve as training grounds for taking on larger risks. Establish a habit of regularly stepping outside your comfort zone, and celebrate these mini-leaps. Over time, your capacity to embrace larger risks will expand, and your confidence in handling discomfort will grow.

Moreover, consider reframing discomfort as an opportunity for excitement. Our brains often elicit similar physiological responses to excitement and fear, making it easy to confuse the two. Train yourself to recognise these feelings as indicators of growth. When facing a risky situation, ask yourself, "What am I excited about in this moment?" This small shift can alter your perception and encourage a more positive approach to risk.

Creating a Safety Net. While embracing risk is essential, it is also prudent to create a safety net. This practice does not signal a retreat from risk, but rather establishes a foundation of stability from which you can leap. A safety net provides the emotional and practical reassurance that, when you take risks, there are measures in place to support you through potential failures.

Begin creating your safety net by identifying your resources. This can include financial savings, a supportive network of friends and family, or alternative plans that you can execute if things do not go as anticipated. Having a backup plan mitigates the fear associated with making bold moves.

Additionally, practice self-care strategies to maintain your mental and emotional well-being. Engage in activities that nourish you: exercise, meditation, art, or anything that brings you joy. A robust support system will cushion the impact of failures, allowing you to recover and return to the pursuit of success with renewed vigour. Visualising Success. One of the most powerful tools in embracing risk is visualisation. Visualisation involves mentally picturing your dreams as if they are already realised. This act not only stimulates motivation but also reinforces your belief in your worthiness of success.

Establish a daily practice of visualisation where you close your eyes and vividly imagine what success looks like for you. Engage all your senses in this practice: how do you feel? What do you see, hear, and smell? By immersing yourself in this mental experience, you begin to embody the state of success, breeding confidence and resilience. Visualisation can also serve as a rehearsal tool for the risks you are preparing to take. Envision the potential obstacles you might face and imagine yourself navigating them successfully. By rehearsing the process, you diminish the element of surprise and anxiety; instead, you equip yourself with strategies to confront whatever comes your way.

Taking Incremental Steps. Embracing risks does not necessitate a grand leap off a cliff; often, it can be achieved through incremental steps. Begin with small, manageable risks that edge you closer to your goals. Each small step serves as a building block, compounding your confidence and fortifying your belief in your abilities.

Set SMART goals—Specific, Measurable, Achievable, Relevant, and Time-bound—that outline actionable steps toward your larger aspirations. The specificity of these goals clarifies the path ahead, making it easier to take the first leap. Celebrate each small victory along the way, reinforcing your momentum and commitment.

It is also essential to be flexible. As you take these steps, remain open to changes in direction. Sometimes the path will shift, revealing new opportunities and challenges. Embracing adaptability not only enhances resilience but also allows you to respond thoughtfully to unforeseen circumstances.

Developing an Action Plan. No leap of faith is complete without a structured action plan. A well-thought-out plan serves to translate your intentions into tangible steps. It organises your thoughts, identifies priorities, and establishes timelines, making it easier to engage meaningfully with your goals.

Begin by breaking down your larger goals into actionable tasks. For instance, if you aspire to start a business, outline the steps involved, such as researching your market, drafting a business plan, securing funding, and launching your product. Each of these components will help structure your process and create manageable chunks of work.

Establish specific timelines for each task to maintain your momentum and stay on track. Deadlines compel us to take action, ensuring that our aspirations remain at the forefront of our priorities. Consistently revisit and adjust your action plan as necessary, reflecting on your progress and refining your approach based on experiences and feedback.

Seeking Mentorship and Guidance. In any venture, seeking guidance from mentors or peers can significantly enhance your capacity to take risks. Connect with individuals who have traversed similar paths and who can offer invaluable insights drawn from their experiences. These relationships can offer you new perspectives and actionable advice tailored to your unique journey.

Mentorship also creates a vital sense of accountability. Sharing your intentions and action plans with someone you trust can encourage you to stay committed to your goals, even in the face of adversity. Constructive feedback from mentors can illuminate blind spots, introducing ideas or strategies that you might not have previously considered.

Additionally, engaging in communities—whether online or locally—of like-minded individuals can foster an environment conducive to exploration and risk-taking. These networks provide support, encouragement, and opportunities for collaboration. They create a safe space where you can share fears, discuss challenges, and celebrate accomplishments.

Reframing Failure as Feedback. As you embark on this journey of risk-taking, it is crucial to adopt a constructive relationship with failure. Failure is not the antithesis of success; instead, it is an inevitable segment of the journey. Every successful figure has endured setbacks, but what separates them from those who do not move forward is their ability to view failure as a learning opportunity.

Practice reframing your perspective on failure. Instead of letting it define you or your worth, extract invaluable lessons from the experience. Ask yourself: What went wrong? What could I do differently next time? By shifting the narrative around failure, you free yourself to continue pursuing your dreams with renewed resolve.

Maintain a failure journal where you document key insights gained from your setbacks. Recognise the growth that occurred through adversity, identifying strengths and skills you've cultivated. This reflective practice can serve as a reminder that failure is simply a stepping stone on the path to success.

Celebrating Successes, Big and Small

No accounting of risk-taking would be complete without acknowledging success. The journey to achieving our dreams is filled with milestones, both large and small. It is essential to celebrate these moments, no matter their magnitude, as they reinforce our belief in our capabilities.

Create a ritual for celebrating successes. It can take varied forms, such as throwing a small gathering, indulging in a favourite treat, or taking a moment to reflect on your achievements. By celebrating, you recognise the progress you've made, fostering an attitude of gratitude and positivity that fuels further risk-taking and success.

Sharing your successes with others can also amplify the joy of your achievements. Inspire those around you by discussing your journey, imparting lessons learned and illustrating the potential of embracing risks. Your experiences can light the path for others, encouraging them to confront their own fears and pursue their aspirations.

Conclusion

Embracing risks is fundamental to overcoming the fear of success and unlocking your potential. By recalibrating your mindset, embracing discomfort, crafting actionable plans, seeking guidance, reframing failure, and celebrating every victory, you pave the way toward your dreams. The most significant leap you will take is the leap of faith in recognising that you are worthy of all the joy and achievement life holds.

These strategies empower you to approach the journey with courage and resilience, enabling you to create a life that reflects your highest aspirations. Let them guide you, compel you, and liberate you from the chains of self-doubt and fear. Embrace the risks inherent in your pursuit, for it is only through them that you will discover the true extent of your potential. Leap into your dreams; the world is waiting for your brilliance.

We Are Our Own Enemies

Pride and Ego

The Masks We Wear

In the journey of self-discovery, the Seeker often finds themselves at a crossroads, reflecting on the complexities of pride and ego. They see these traits as but two masks worn by individuals in various facets of life, obscuring authenticity and connection. It is in this elusive dance of self that The Seeker begins to understand the profound impact of pride and ego on relationships—not only with oneself but also with others.

At a glance, pride can be perceived as a sense of self-worth and personal value. In moderation, it can serve as a source of motivation, fuelling ambition and encouraging individuals to strive for success. However, The Seeker has learned that unchecked pride morphs into arrogance, creating barriers that alienate rather than connect. It becomes a shield, a mask that protects the vulnerability hidden beneath. Yet, masks can be deceiving; they can conceal flaws, insecurities, and fears, allowing the ego to take centre stage.

The Seeker recalls an instance in their life when pride shone brightly. It was during a particularly successful project at work—one that had garnered attention and praise from colleagues and superiors alike. Basking in the limelight, The Seeker indulged in the accolades, slowly slipping into a state of inflated self-importance. In that moment, soaring high on the wings of success, they lost sight of the collaborative spirit that had birthed the achievement. Team members who once contributed valuable insights felt diminished, overshadowed by The Seeker's unwavering focus on personal glory.

As time passed, The Seeker witnessed the effects of their unchecked ego. Relationships within the team began to fray. Communication dwindled, and once-vibrant brainstorming sessions grew muted. The palpable distance escalated tension and resentment, creating an environment rife with suspicion and defensiveness. The Seeker's pride had become a barrier, distancing them from their peers, eroding the foundations of trust and collaboration.

In observing these dynamics, The Seeker reflects on the paradox of pride: it promises affirmation yet threatens isolation. They find comfort in the acknowledgment of their shortcomings, determined to reclaim humility as a guiding principle. But as they begin to peel away the layers of ego, they encounter societal pressures that inflame pride, complicating their journey toward self-awareness and authentic connection.

In nearly every corner of society, the message is clear: success and worthiness are measured by external validation and accolades. From social media platforms to corporate ladder rankings, individuals are burdened with the expectation to flaunt their accomplishments and present polished images of themselves. The Seeker contemplates how the relentless pursuit of admiration intensifies the ego's grip, often leading one to adopt a façade that betrays their true self.

This societal lens distorts personal worth, perpetuating a cycle wherein individuals feel compelled to wear masks that often clash with their intrinsic values. The Seeker is acutely aware that by prioritizing the validation of others, they sacrifice the authenticity that fosters meaningful relationships. In their pursuit of connection, they realize that humility is not a sign of weakness but rather an acknowledgment of one's imperfections—an invitation for others to step into the light of shared humanity.

The Seeker's journey leads them to confront the manifestations of pride and ego they encounter within themselves and those around them. They explore the narratives held by friends, family, and the broader community. It becomes evident that pride can evoke a sense of superiority, pushing individuals to dismiss the contributions and worth of others. The Seeker recognizes this as a cycle that perpetuates division and inhibits true collaboration.

With each reflection, the Seeker finds themselves facing uncomfortable truths. They begin to question their own behaviour in social situations—were they truly listening to others, or merely waiting for an opportunity to share their thoughts? Were they genuinely curious about the experiences of those around them, or were they more invested in projecting their persona? As The Seeker navigates these revelations, they realize the fragility of human connection. The masks we wear can guard against vulnerability, but they can also suffocate our relationships. When ego takes precedence, communication turns into a transaction, a contest of who can articulate their points better rather than a dialogue of mutual understanding. The Seeker's resolve to embrace humility becomes a commitment to fostering deeper connections, to genuinely listening and valuing the perspectives of others.

And so, The Seeker embarks on a path toward cultivating humility in their interactions. They understand that true connection stems from a willingness to lower one's defences, creating space for authenticity. In doing so, The Seeker discovers that humility is not synonymous with self-deprecation; rather, it's the recognition of one's worth alongside the worth of others. It's an appreciation for the diverse gifts and perspectives everyone brings to the table.

As much as The Seeker craves this connection, they cannot ignore the resistance that arises when faced with the prospect of letting go of pride. The fear of vulnerability looms large, whispering a familiar refrain: "You must protect yourself. You need to ensure you don't appear weak." It is in these moments of inner struggle that The Seeker channels their attention back to the transformative power of humility. They reflect on how humility fosters an environment where individuals feel safe enough to lower their masks, free from the pressures of judgment.

Real change begins with The Seeker's commitment to practice humility in daily interactions—small conversations with friends, family, and colleagues. They strive to listen with intentionality, to ask questions that invite others to share their stories, and to respect differing opinions without feeling threatened. In this pursuit, The Seeker finds that the ego begins to retreat, slowly yielding space for empathy and understanding.

The Seeker longs for a society where individuals are not merely celebrated for their achievements but are recognized for their integrity, compassion, and ability to uplift others. They imagine a world where pride is balanced by humility, a community that faces its challenges collectively rather than competitively. Yet, the lingering questions remain: How can this shift be achieved in a world that constantly inflates egos? How can we encourage authentic connections amidst societal pressures?

The Seeker's reflections lead them to explore narratives that exemplify triumphs of humility over pride. They discover stories of leaders who, despite their achievements, remained grounded in their mission to serve others. They learn of communities that prioritize collaboration over competition, celebrating collective success rather than individual accolades. These stories inspire The Seeker, igniting a desire not only to embody humility but also to encourage it in others.

Yet the task is not without its challenges. The Seeker knows they must confront the discomfort that arises when pride is called into question. They must allow themselves to feel vulnerable, to embrace the uncertainty that accompanies shedding old patterns. This is the crucible of transformation—the willingness to face one's inner battles and recognize the masks that shield the soul from authentic relationships.

Before long, The Seeker reaches a pivotal moment of realization. They understand that the journey toward humility and away from pride is not linear; it is intricate and filled with setbacks. It requires ongoing reflection, self-awareness, and a commitment to personal growth. The Seeker reminds themselves that struggles are part of the process, and embracing discomfort is key to dismantling the ego's stronghold.

Armed with this understanding, The Seeker begins to cultivate new practices that ground them in humility. They engage in self-reflection through journaling, taking time to evaluate their responses in various situations. When encountering conflicts, they speak to others with openness, acknowledging their contributions and recognizing the value of shared experiences. It is in these honest conversations that The Seeker senses the freedom that comes from unmasking the ego—the release of burdens that had long weighed them down.

The Seeker becomes a beacon for those around them, encouraging friends and colleagues to embark on their own journeys of self-discovery. They create a safe environment for discussion, championing the idea that vulnerability is strength. In embracing humility, The Seeker witnesses the ripple effect, as others begin to lower their masks and engage in deeper conversations—conversations that foster empathy, collaboration, and a renewed sense of community.

We Are Our Own Enemies

As they forge ahead, The Seeker acknowledges the ongoing challenge of societal expectations and pressures that often inflate the ego. It is an uphill battle, but they remain resolute. They engage in dialogues about the importance of redefining success—expanding the definition beyond the accumulation of accolades and riches to include kindness, collaboration, and connection.

In their tireless quest for authenticity, The Seeker delves into the roles that culture and values play in shaping perceptions of pride. They analyse how societal narratives can fuel egotism while recognizing influential voices that emphasize humility and cooperation. By sharing these insights with others, The Seeker aims to foster a broader understanding of the importance of collective identity over individual achievement.

Ultimately, the Seeker's journey leads them to a profound realization: the masks we wear are not inherently bad but are reflections of the complexities of human nature. Each mask has its purpose, serving as both a protective barrier and a potential hindrance to authentic connection. The key lies in the conscious choice of when to don a mask—and when to set it aside.

The balance between pride and humility becomes an ongoing dialogue throughout The Seeker's life. They accept that the ego may never fully disappear, but the goal is to keep it in check. It is in this dynamic tension that The Seeker finds a sense of peace, recognizing that they are a work in progress, constantly evolving and learning from every encounter.

As The Seeker continues to strip away the layers of pride and ego, they ultimately find solace in connecting with others who share similar struggles. They invite individuals from all walks of life to engage in conversations about their journeys, emphasizing that everyone grapples with wearing masks. Through shared stories and experiences, a newfound sense of community emerges—one that cherishes vulnerability and mutual understanding.

In the heart of this community lies an innate recognition of the power of humility. The Seeker becomes a champion for authentic connection, encouraging others to join in the transformative path toward unmasking their true selves. This journey is not merely an individual endeavour but a collective one, fostering an environment where relationships are nurtured and compassion reigns supreme.

The Seeker understands that pride and ego may perpetually seek to assert themselves, stirring up doubt and uncertainty. Yet, they arm themselves with the knowledge that acknowledging these emotions is the first step toward transcending them. The choice to wear humility rather than pride becomes an intentional act—one that holds the promise of forging deeper connections with oneself and others.

In learning to embrace both the beauty in their flaws and the strengths of others, The Seeker embarks on a renewed commitment to a life marked by authenticity, vulnerability, and connection. They know that true success lies not in the accolades that dazzle the eye but in fostering relationships that nourish the soul, crafting a tapestry woven from shared experiences, laughter, and compassion. Such is the journey of unmasking the ego and embracing the beauty of being human.

Vulnerability and Connection

In a world that often equates strength with the ability to put up walls, to be seen as invulnerable, and to showcase a perfect façade, the notion of vulnerability can feel daunting. It stands in stark contrast to pride and ego, qualities that many cherish as hallmarks of success. Yet, what if vulnerability is not a sign of weakness but a profound source of strength? What if by embracing our vulnerabilities, we could foster deeper connections, create more meaningful relationships, and ultimately, free ourselves from the shackles of pride?

As we embark on this exploration, it's crucial to reframe our understanding of vulnerability. Contrary to the conventional wisdom that might label it as a liability, vulnerability is the catalyst for authentic connection. It is through our vulnerabilities that we reveal our true selves, allowing others to see us, not just our polished exteriors. When we peel back the layers of pride and ego, we expose the beautifully imperfect, raw, and real aspects of who we are. Herein lies the paradox: to truly connect with others, we must first dare to be seen in our most exposed and unguarded states.

Consider the story of two friends, Sarah and Mia. Both women appeared to have it all together from the outside—successful careers, thriving social lives, and seemingly happy families. Yet, neither shared the struggles they experienced behind the scenes. Sarah wrestled with anxiety and feelings of inadequacy, while Mia battled crippling loneliness despite her active social life. Both women felt isolated in their struggles, believing that revealing their inner turmoil would appear as a weakness to the other. They maintained a façade, engaging in casual conversations that glossed over their deeper issues.

One day, during a coffee date, Sarah finally exposed her vulnerability. She spoke about her anxiety and the continuous battle to feel enough. As she opened up, she felt a wave of relief; the weight she carried began to lift. To her surprise, Mia listened intently, her own eyes welling up with tears. For the first time, Mia shared her experiences of loneliness, her fear of being alone, and her longing for genuine connection. In that moment, pride dissolved, and vulnerability became the bond that not only deepened their friendship but illuminated a path toward healing. This simple yet profound interaction illustrates the transformative power of sharing our vulnerabilities. By allowing ourselves to be seen, we widened the space for empathy, understanding, and connection. Vulnerability invites others to show up raw and real, creating a safe environment where both parties can embrace their imperfections without fear of judgment. In contrast, pride often builds walls that leave us disconnected, scared to express our true feelings, or worried about how we will be perceived.

Embracing vulnerability does not mean we should wear our hearts on our sleeves indiscriminately. Instead, it involves choosing authenticity over the comfort of maintaining a façade. It requires a level of discernment about whom to trust with our truth. Vulnerability is about sharing our authentic selves with those who can hold space for us, accepting us without judgment. Through this lens, we can see how vulnerability enriches relationships at multiple layers. Most importantly, it fosters trust. When we open up about our struggles, fears, and insecurities, we signal to others that it is safe to do the same. Trust breeds connection, and connection fosters community. When we are vulnerable, we create a culture in our relationships where honesty flourishes, and authenticity is celebrated.

Moreover, by admitting our fears and imperfections, we invite the grace of acceptance into our relationships. Vulnerability shatters the illusion of perfection, allowing us to lean into our shared humanity. It reminds us that no one is alone in their suffering; that we all walk a similar path of challenges and struggles, despite each person's unique circumstances. As we acknowledge our imperfections, we pave the way for true intimacy, knowing that our flaws make us uniquely human.

We Are Our Own Enemies

Exploring the paradox of pride reveals that the ego often operates under the illusion that being "perfect" will garner respect and admiration. Yet, the opposite rings true. It is our imperfections that make us relatable. People do not connect with the polished version of ourselves; they see themselves reflected in our shared struggles. When ego drives our interactions, we risk operating in isolation, leading to loneliness. Pride seduces us into believing that we must present a flawless image. As we shed this need for perfection, we can embark on a journey of connection through vulnerability.

Research has shown that vulnerability can manifest as a form of emotional courage, a concept championed by Brené Brown, an expert in the field of social work and vulnerability research. Brown asserts that vulnerability is the birthplace of innovation, creativity, and change. She invites us to think of vulnerability as "the willingness to show up and be seen, to ask for what we need, to talk about how we feel." This courage to be vulnerable directly correlates with deeper, more meaningful connections with others. When we embrace our emotional bravery, we not only enrich our relationships but also cultivate resilience within ourselves.

But how do we move from understanding the importance of vulnerability to practicing it in our everyday lives? It requires intentionality and courage. Practicing vulnerability can begin with small steps. Engage in conversations where you share a recent struggle or a personal story that invites your listener to connect. Open up to a trusted friend about a fear you have been harbouring. Create safe spaces where vulnerability is welcomed and celebrated instead of met with judgment or dismissal.

Another profound avenue for exploring vulnerability lies in practicing self-compassion. To show up authentically for others, we must first cultivate a nourishing relationship with ourselves. Embrace your imperfections and treat yourself with kindness when you stumble. Self-compassion allows us to experience vulnerability without spiralling into self-judgment. When we are gentle with ourselves, it becomes easier to extend grace to others, fostering deeper connections.

The act of writing or journaling can also serve as a vehicle for vulnerability. Putting pen to paper can help clarify your thoughts and feelings, allowing you to explore areas where pride might be holding you back. By engaging with your inner dialogue, you can identify moments where you've felt pressured to present a façade, and subsequently refocus on embracing your authentic self. This reflective practice can equip you with the insights necessary to approach conversations with vulnerability.

In conversations, consider employing active listening techniques—empowering both yourself and others to engage with vulnerability. By listening deeply to what someone else is sharing, you create an atmosphere of safety. It is not merely about waiting for your turn to speak but genuinely seeking to understand the other person's perspective. This responsiveness paves the way for deeper discussions and a mutual exchange of vulnerabilities.

For many, the fear of judgment looms large when discussing personal matters. Remember that people often project their insecurities onto others. When you take that courageous step to be vulnerable, you may inspire others to follow suit, transforming what could have been a moment of isolation into a shared experience. It is important to recognize that while not everyone may respond positively, the right relationships will foster an environment where vulnerability is met with respect and understanding.

Building on these ideas, cultivating empathy becomes essential in nurturing connections rooted in vulnerability. Seek to approach interactions with curiosity rather than judgment. When we understand that everyone is fighting their own battles, we can approach others with kindness. Empathy acts as a bridge—a way for us to connect more profoundly by showing concern, understanding, and support for one another without falling prey to ego-driven assumptions.

As our relationships blossom through vulnerability and connection, we should not forget the power of community. Many of us isolate ourselves in our struggles. Finding spaces such as support groups, therapy sessions, or community centres can provide us with the chance to engage with others who may be experiencing similar challenges. These connections remind us that our narratives are often echoed by others, creating a tapestry of shared experience that demystifies the burdens of pride.

As we conclude this exploration, we must remember that embracing vulnerability is a continuous journey. It is not a destination but rather a courageous practice that can change our lives in remarkable ways. As pride diminishes its grip on our interactions, we find deeper connections waiting on the other side. The act of letting go of the need for perfection not only fosters unity among individuals, enriches relationships, and creates communities grounded in empathy, but it also prepares the ground for healing and transformation.

When we shift our perspective to view vulnerability as a source of strength, we embrace the fullness of being alive—frailty, resilience, connection, and love. In a world where we often battle against our inner adversaries, inviting vulnerability to the forefront awakens the power to redefine how we connect with ourselves and others. The paradox of pride fades as we expose our vulnerabilities, creating a more profound symbiotic relationship with both ourselves and those around us.

Let us strive to embark on this journey together, choosing vulnerability as our strength and recognizing that the courage to be seen opens the door to the rich world of connection that lies just beyond the veil of pride. In doing so, we reclaim not only our authenticity but also the collective joy of shared humanity—a source of profound transformation that reinforces the belief that we indeed are most powerful when we dare to be vulnerable.

Healing Through Reconciliation

Pride and ego often serve as formidable barriers in our relationships, creating chasms where there should be connection and warmth. When we allow our inflated self-worth or the need to be right to govern our interactions, we unintentionally push others away. This chapter will delve into the importance of healing through reconciliation, offering a guide to navigating the inner dialogues essential for mending fractured connections.

Reconciliation is an intricate process, more than a simple apology or acknowledgment of wrongdoing; it requires sincere effort, humility, and a willingness to step beyond our pride. While it may take courage to reach out to someone we've hurt or who has hurt us, healing begins the moment we decide to forgo our ego in favour of understanding. This decision lays the groundwork for rebuilding trust and forging deeper connections.

To embark on this journey of reconciliation, we must first cultivate the inner dialogues that will guide us. These conversations often begin within our own hearts and minds, fostering self-awareness and prompting us to reflect on our attitudes, behaviours, and motivations. Here are key aspects to consider when assessing our role in conflict and the path toward healing.

The first step is acknowledging the impact of pride on our relationships. Pride often masquerades as confidence, but it can quickly turn toxic when it obstructs genuine communication. Recognizing when pride prevails in our interactions allows us to shift our focus from self-centeredness to empathy. It is essential to ask ourselves: What triggered my reaction? Was it a need to protect my self-image or an opportunity to express understanding?

This self-reflection lays a strong foundation for fostering dialogue. It invites vulnerability and openness, qualities that can be powerful in promoting reconciliation. When we view ourselves honestly, we create space for conversations that may feel uncomfortable but are necessary for healing. Acknowledging our faults does not diminish our worth; rather, it shows a commitment to personal growth and a desire to enhance our relationships.

As we examine our motivations, another key element involves developing empathy. Stepping into another person's shoes enriches our understanding of their experiences and emotions. It transforms the narrative from "them against us" to "we're in this together." This is particularly potent when dealing with fractured relationships, where one person's pride may have silenced another's voice. By encouraging ourselves to listen genuinely, we begin to build bridges rather than walls—a critical component of reconciliation.

Approaching reconciliation also requires sincere acknowledgment of our faults. This might manifest in the form of a heartfelt apology. A sincere apology addresses the hurt caused, takes responsibility for one's actions, and expresses a commitment to change. It is essential to approach this step with authenticity. A mere acknowledgment delivered out of obligation can further alienate others. Instead, we must convey our genuine remorse for causing pain, thereby laying the groundwork for trust to take root once more.

Reaching out to those we've lost connection with can be daunting, especially when our inner critic or pride attempts to hold us back. We may fear rejection or a negative response, but it is vital to remember that reconciliation begins with one courageous step. When we choose to reach out, we not only signal our desire and commitment to mend the relationship, but we also empower ourselves to navigate the outcome with grace. In opening that line of communication, we can use "I" statements to express how we feel. Phrasing our thoughts in this manner minimizes defensiveness and fosters an environment where both parties can express themselves freely. For instance, "I felt hurt when..." or "I regret that my actions led to..." shifts the focus from blame to personal responsibility. This method promotes healing because it acknowledges harm while fostering an atmosphere conducive to reconciliation.

As we continue along the journey of heartfelt reconnection, we need to practice active listening. This means more than simply hearing the words of others; it requires us to engender an open mindset, free from judgment. Engaging with empathy reinforces our commitment to understanding. We cultivate compassion for others, which softens our own hearts, allowing love and connection to flourish.

An essential component of this healing process is addressing the issues at their core. While suppressing feelings may feel easier, it often ignites resentment. Discussing grievances openly allows us to clarify misunderstandings and clear the air. Each conversation can serve as a stepping stone toward honesty and transparency—elements crucial for rebuilding trust.

We Are Our Own Enemies

Encouraging mutual dialogue fosters reconciliation and transforms it into a two-way street. It's crucial not only to share our thoughts and feelings but to create an inviting space for others to do the same. Each person's voice matters; this reciprocation assures us that healing is not only possible but also attainable. Building on these dialogues, we can devise practical solutions that ensure healthier interactions. Creating mutual agreements on behaviour can help solidify the principles upon which new relationships can thrive. For example, deciding to check in with one another regularly or establishing boundaries can facilitate better communication. Clarity on these points diminishes future misunderstandings and helps nurture a nurturing space for both parties involved.

Part of the healing journey also involves the process of forgiveness—not only forgiving others but also ourselves. The weight of holding onto resentment can impede our growth and impact our overall well-being. When we embrace forgiveness, we unlock the chains of bitterness that bind us and, crucially, allow love to fill the spaces once occupied by hurt. This act does not mean condoning the actions of another but rather releasing the emotional burden we carry.

Forgiveness is often challenging, particularly when pride urges us to hold onto grievances. However, recognizing the importance of forgiveness in our healing opens pathways to personal freedom. It enables us to reclaim our power, directing it towards our own growth and well-being rather than feeding an endless cycle of animosity.

As we strive for reconciliation, we must practice patience. Healing is not an instantaneous process but a gradual unfolding of understanding and connection. At times, we may encounter setbacks. Trust, once broken, takes time to rebuild. Nevertheless, cultivating perseverance in our efforts strengthens both our character and our relationships. Each small act of kindness and understanding reinforces our journey toward healing.

This path to reconciliation not only fosters personal relationships but has the potential to shape the broader communities we are part of. Healing begins at the individual level but resonates outward, influencing our interactions within families, workplaces, and beyond. When we commit to building bridges instead of isolating divisions, we contribute to a culture of understanding and collaboration, elevating the collective experience.

In conclusion, the path to healing through reconciliation is a journey that challenges us to confront our pride and ego. By engaging in genuine inner dialogues, acknowledging faults, reaching out, and fostering empathy, we create opportunities for shared healing. It is through this process that we move beyond mere coexistence into deep, authentic connections. As we embrace the principles of forgiveness, active listening, and open communication, we not only heal the fractures within our relationships but also pave the way for our shared humanity to flourish. Reconciliation is not simply about repairing what was broken; it is about co-creating a future defined by compassion, understanding, and powerful ties that can withstand the trials of pride. In each act of healing, we uncover the possibility of transformation—not just for ourselves, but for everyone we encounter.

Manipulation and Control

The Hidden Dynamics

In the quiet corners of our lives, there exists a force that often goes unnoticed, weaving its way through our interactions and relationships. This force is manipulation, a dynamic that can so subtly disguise itself as care, concern, or even love. Many of us have experienced it, perhaps without fully recognizing the implications it carries. I certainly have, and in these pages, I invite you to walk with me through a personal journey, delving into the hidden dynamics of manipulation as it has manifested in my life. Let us uncover how it can masquerade as support and affection, ultimately becoming a barrier to authentic connection.

I remember a time in my life when I thought I was surrounded by individuals who truly cared for me. They offered their guidance, their opinions, and their judgments wrapped meticulously in words of love. "I'm only looking out for you," they would say, their eyes filled with what I now recognize as a controlling fire disguised as concern. At that moment, I felt validated, embraced in a cocoon of apparent safety, blissfully unaware that the very nurturing I craved was masking a subtle ensnarement.

In my early twenties, I had a close friend named Sarah. We met in college, and our connection felt immediate. She was vivacious, spirited, and always full of ideas and dreams. I admired her ability to articulate her thoughts and feelings with poise, a quality that drew me in. Over time, however, her charms began to reveal an underlying layer of manipulation. It started innocuously enough with her advice. She would suggest what to wear to parties, how to style my hair, and which classes to take, all wrapped in a sweet, persuasive tone.

We Are Our Own Enemies

"You just want to fit in," she would tell me with a laugh, "Let me help you with that." At first, I relished her company and welcomed her contributions. But soon enough, I found myself walking in her shadow, my own voice dwindling beneath the weight of her expectations. What had begun as a friendship slowly morphed into a hierarchy, with her at the apex. My identity began to blur, and I often found myself questioning my choices.

As a seeker of validation, I realized how easily it became to mistake manipulation for genuine care. I would convince myself that her ways were out of a desire for my happiness. After all, who better to guide me through my formative years than someone who seemed to know what they were talking about? Yet in moments of decision-making—whether they revolved around personal relationships or academic pursuits—I would feel an unsettling pressure that instinctively pointed toward her preferences rather than my own. In moments when I needed affirmation, I instead received subtle directives cloaked in the guise of friendship.

One day, during a low point in my academic journey, I reached out to Sarah for help. I had failed an important exam, and my emotional vulnerability was at an all-time high. "You know you could have studied harder, right?" she said, her voice sharp enough to cut through my self-doubt. "We could have set up study sessions if you really cared." The weight of her words hung heavy in the air, a fabric woven from concern and blame. I walked away feeling crushed, confused by the notion that her criticism, however cleverly disguised as guidance, was a reflection of her own insecurities. In the days that followed, I began to examine the nature of our relationship. Had I dismissed my intuition for too long? Was I so eager to feel taken care of that I ignored the signs that something was off? The moments I had initially seen as supportive began to take on a chilling light. Instead of empowering me, Sarah's influence often left me adrift, unsure of who I was outside the contours of her expectations.

Exploring this dynamic further, I found myself reflecting on the interaction between manipulation and vulnerability. It is a delicate dance; those who manipulate often prey on the very insecurities we carry. They position themselves as the saviours, the ones offering the proverbial life raft amidst turbulent waters. In doing so, they secure their influence over us, compelling us to depend on their perceived wisdom.

There are moments when this dynamic plays out in the most innocent ways. During a family gathering not long after my introspections about Sarah, I overheard a conversation between my relatives. As they discussed plans for the upcoming holiday, I felt a familiar tug of obligation. "You should definitely come home for Christmas," my mother said, the urgency in her voice palpable. "It'll be so good for you to be around the family."

Her intentions were coated in love, undoubtedly, but as I listened more closely, I could sense an underlying edge of guilt. "You need to reconnect with your roots." My heart sank a little. I had plans that year; a trip I had been looking forward to for months. Yet, the guilt stemming from her manipulation—falling under the guise of familial affection—made my resolve waver.

As I navigated these family dynamics, I realized that manipulation transcends singular relationships. It can be a thread woven through familial ties, friendships, and even professional environments. In many contexts, affection offers the perfect cover for manipulation to flourish, making it even harder to recognize. It often masquerades as advice, concern, or even love. In truth, the unexamined intention behind such messages can derail authentic connection.

We Are Our Own Enemies

When we derive our identity based on others' perceptions or regressive judgments, we lose sight of our authentic selves. In my case, rather than pursuing my own path, I was drifting into a sea of expectations that were not my own. As humans, we yearn to anchor our identities in genuine connections, yet our fears and vulnerabilities can leave us susceptible to those who wield manipulation as a tool.

Another embryonic instance of manipulation came not from a friend or family member but from my employer. My job had driven me to my limits, and in moments of exhaustion, I was always greeted by words meant to pacify. "You're doing great! Just hang in there a little longer," my manager would say, while we both knew the workload was becoming untenable. While she portrayed it as encouragement, it felt like a cushion for the inevitable burnout—a strategy to tame my frustration without addressing the root of the problem.

My dissatisfaction grew, burdened further by a skewed sense of loyalty. The manipulation was not overt; it was intertwined with a semblance of care. "We value you, and your hard work is noticed," she would say, yet the reality was that my contributions had become the expectation, a marker of how well I could meet relentless demands. It felt as if part of me was being chipped away—a slow erosion coated with hollow praise.

Over time, I began to realize that manipulation often finds its home in relationships marked by fear. Fear of inadequacy, disappointment, and confrontation can create a landscape where individuals feel compelled to play roles that align with others' expectations. This was deeply rooted in my experiences—I had allowed those around me to dictate my reactions, thus further perpetuating their control.

We Are Our Own Enemies

It took years of introspection for me to grasp the true nature of manipulation. I learned to distinguish between someone genuinely looking out for my best interests and someone who used my vulnerabilities as leverage. It sparked a hunger for authentic connections, free from masks and veils. I began to cultivate friendships where I felt secure in voicing my feelings, even if they churned with discomfort.

Therapeutic insights guided me toward understanding how the narratives we embrace often affect our interpersonal connections. I learned to set boundaries, an essential armour against the hidden dynamics of manipulation. Creating emotional distance is not an act of selfishness; rather, it is a necessary step toward reclaiming autonomy in our relationships. Only when I began to place trust in my own voice could I advocate for healthier dynamics.

Martin, a mentor I encountered years later, became a beacon of support in my journey. He emphasized the importance of open communication, validating my feelings as a foundation for meaningful connection. "True care," he would say, "is grounded in honest dialogue. It allows space for vulnerabilities without masquerading as something else." His insights reshaped my understanding of relationships, guiding me to redefine what authentic connection truly meant.

Navigating relationships requires vigilance and awareness of the subtle dance of manipulation that can occur at any juncture. Recognizing its existence often forces us to confront our insecurities—the triggers that create fertile ground for controlling dynamics. Each time I've encountered manipulation, I've been presented with a choice: to succumb to its grip or challenge the narrative that binds me to others' expectations.

We Are Our Own Enemies

Eventually, I learned to advocate for my needs, expressing my discomfort and aligning my choices with my own values. As I began to voice my desires and hesitations clearly, I noticed a shift in my relationships. It became apparent how the dynamics began to shift not just with Sarah, my manager, or family members, but also with friendships I had once perceived as supportive. The more I asserted my authenticity, the less likely I was to accept a distorted version of concern.

The journey to unmask manipulation is fraught with challenge. In a world that so often promotes image over authenticity, it's easy to find ourselves losing sight of our own values. Yet, as I navigated these encounters, I came to an empowering realization that the strongest relationships are built upon trust, honesty, and shared values. They flourish when we stand firm in our own truth, unapologetically presenting our whole selves without fear of being overshadowed.

The dynamics of manipulation are an intricate tapestry woven into the fabric of human interaction. Its subtleties can be particularly sneaky, often evolving into a barrier that stifles authentic connection and emotional intimacy. It calls on us to remain vigilant, to sift through the layers of care and concern, in search of the truths that reside beneath.

As I pen these words, I hope to emerge not just as a voice of caution but one that inspires empowerment. Understanding manipulation's true nature offers us the opportunity to keep our connections authentic, balanced, and filled with genuine care. Ultimately, the journey is about building trust in ourselves and fostering relationships grounded in empowerment rather than control. Only then can we break through the false façades that manipulation casts, stepping into the light of authentic connections that allow us to thrive.

Recognizing Manipulation

Manipulation, often ensconced in layers of charm or feigned concern, can be deceptively subtle, making it one of the most insidious forms of control in personal relationships. To recognize and resist it effectively, we must first understand the tactics used by manipulators and the dynamics they create. This subchapter aims to illuminate these behaviours, arming you with the knowledge to identify red flags and assess your relationships critically.

Manipulators often employ various tactics, each designed to shift the balance of power in their favour. One of the most common is emotional blackmail. This involves leveraging fear, obligation, and guilt to control another's behaviour. For instance, a partner might say, "If you really loved me, you would do this for me," implying that your love is conditional upon meeting their demands. Emotional blackmail can induce a state of constant anxiety, leading you to question your feelings and, ultimately, your worth within the relationship.

Another prevalent tactic is gaslighting, named after a classic play in which a husband manipulates his wife into doubting her sanity. In personal relationships, gaslighting can manifest through persistent denial of facts or distorting reality. A manipulator might dismiss your recollections of events, claiming you are "overreacting" or "making things up." Over time, this can erode your self-confidence and exacerbate feelings of confusion. Recognizing gaslighting involves paying attention to how you feel after interacting with someone. If you frequently doubt your perceptions or feel like you're "walking on eggshells," these could be signs of an emotionally manipulative relationship.

We Are Our Own Enemies

Withdrawing affection or attention is another tactic manipulator use to maintain control. This behaviour, often termed the "silent treatment," serves to punish or coerce the other person into compliance. For example, suppose your partner becomes cold or disinterested when you express a differing opinion. In that case, they create an imbalance that leads you to modify your views just to regain their approval. The silent treatment can induce feelings of loneliness and desperation, making you more inclined to placate the manipulator in future conflicts.

The use of flattery or love bombing can mask true intentions, another hallmark of manipulative relationships. Initially, the manipulator may shower you with compliments and affection, creating a false sense of security. This can often disarm your defences, making you less vigilant about their subsequent controlling behaviours. Once you are emotionally invested, the real manipulation begins. This tactic is particularly pernicious as it intertwines genuine affection with ulterior motives, complicating your ability to discern where genuine love ends and manipulation begins.

Another red flag to be aware of is the constant need for validation and support from one party, often at the expense of the other. In a healthy relationship, both partners should freely share and support each other. However, if one partner consistently demands emotional labour without reciprocation, it might indicate a manipulative dynamic. This person may use guilt to manipulate their partner into fulfilling their emotional needs, leading to feelings of inadequacy or resentment.

Moreover, frequent boundary violations can signify manipulation. Respecting personal boundaries is essential in any relationship, yet manipulators often view boundaries as obstacles to control. For example, suppose you consistently express discomfort with certain topics but the other person continues to push you. In that case, this disregard not only illustrates manipulative behaviour but also serves as a clear sign of emotional disrespect. Recognizing and asserting your boundaries is vital in these scenarios to safeguard your emotional health.

Projecting insecurity onto you is yet another tactic employed by manipulators. This behaviour involves the manipulator deflecting their doubts and fears onto you, leading you to question your stability and self-esteem. A classic manifestation of this is when a partner, feeling insecure, continually questions your fidelity or commitment, projecting their insecurities onto you to create a false narrative that justifies their controlling behaviour. If you find yourself in a cycle of defending your choices or feelings rather than discussing mutual concerns, this may indicate projection at play.

Another important aspect to consider is the relational dynamic of blame and shame. Manipulative individuals often refuse to acknowledge their shortcomings, instead placing the burden of responsibility on their partners. A classic example involves a partner who, when confronted with their passive-aggressive behaviour, responds by saying, "If you weren't so sensitive, I wouldn't have to act this way." Such shifting of blame creates a toxic environment where the manipulator avoids personal accountability while relegating their partner to a constant position of guilt and responsibility.

Recognizing these behaviours requires a combination of self-awareness and external observation. It's essential to reflect on your feelings and responses within your relationships. Are you frequently anxious or defensive around certain individuals? Do you often find yourself justifying their behaviour to others? Observing patterns in how you communicate and feel can provide critical insights into the dynamics at play.

It is equally important to seek the perspectives of trusted friends or family members. Sometimes, those outside the situation can observe dynamics more clearly than we can ourselves. If you confide in a friend and they express concern or discomfort with your relationship, take heed of their observations. An external viewpoint can often help illuminate manipulative patterns you may have normalized.

Keep a journal to track your feelings and interactions. Writing down your experiences can provide clarity, offering a tangible record of manipulative behaviours you have encountered. This practice can also help you recognize recurring themes and triggers, empowering you to address issues with greater confidence when they arise.

Education and awareness are key tools in recognizing manipulation. Reading or engaging with resources that explore healthy relationship dynamics can bolster your understanding of what constitutes emotional toxicity. Books, workshops, or counselling can equip you with the skills to identify and articulate unhealthy patterns, ultimately forcing a re-evaluation of your current circumstances.

Once you've begun to recognize manipulation in your relationships, reflecting on your participation in these dynamics is crucial. Are there aspects of your behaviour that have inadvertently enabled manipulation? Recognizing your role does not equate to accepting blame; rather, it allows for growth and healing. Engaging in self-reflection and counselling can foster personal growth and facilitate healthier relationships in the future.

We Are Our Own Enemies

A key component in recognizing manipulation is understanding your emotional boundaries. Practicing assertiveness and self-care serves to both protect you from manipulative behaviours and reinforce your sense of self-worth. Begin by identifying what makes you feel safe and respected in relationships, then communicate these boundaries clearly and confidently. By doing so, you create criteria through which to gauge the people in your life, thus steering clear of manipulative influences.

Empowerment stems from knowledge. Educating yourself about the mechanics of manipulation can allow you to act more consciously. Familiarize yourself with the characteristics of healthy relationships, focusing on mutual respect, open communication, and consent. Setting these standards for yourself will enable you to evaluate your relationships more effectively, fostering resilience against controlling behaviours.

Furthermore, recognizing manipulation calls for the cultivation of emotional intelligence. Developing skills such as empathy, self-regulation, and social awareness helps you navigate complex emotional landscapes. By enhancing your understanding of both your emotions and those of others, you empower yourself to recognize and address potential manipulative behaviours proactively.

Cultivating a supportive network can also serve as a protective barrier against manipulation. Surround yourself with relationships based on trust, open communication, and mutual support. These relationships provide a foundation where you can freely express your emotions and thoughts without fear of judgment or manipulation. Invest in connections that uplift you, offering a counterbalance to any manipulative influences in your life.

We Are Our Own Enemies

When you begin to identify manipulative behaviours, it is essential to confront them thoughtfully. Addressing manipulation can be complex, as it often involves difficult conversations. Start by expressing your feelings and perceptions directly, using "I" statements to communicate your experiences without appearing accusatory. For example, saying, "I feel uneasy when you say things that contradict our earlier discussions," opens up a dialogue without provoking a defensive reaction.

Dealing with manipulation often requires setting and maintaining firm boundaries. While this can be challenging, especially if someone resists or attempts to redefine your limits, standing your ground is crucial. The ability to assert your boundaries can significantly influence the dynamics of the relationship, prompting a re-evaluation on the part of the manipulator. Remember that healthy relationships thrive on mutual respect, and asserting your boundaries is a fundamental aspect of that respect.

In some cases, if manipulation persists or escalates, it may be necessary to re-evaluate your relationship with that individual. It can be painful to recognize that someone may not have your best interests at heart, but prioritizing your mental and emotional well-being is paramount. Sometimes, distancing yourself from toxic relationships becomes necessary to ensure your personal growth and healing.

As you work to navigate the complexities of relationships marked by manipulation, consider seeking professional guidance. Therapists or counsellors who specialize in relational dynamics can provide valuable insights, helping you not only recognize manipulation but also develop effective strategies for managing it. They can empower you with tools that promote emotional health, resilience, and improved communication.

Empowerment lies at the heart of overcoming manipulative dynamics in relationships. By understanding the tactics used by manipulators and equipping yourself with knowledge, you're better positioned to identify red flags and assess whether your relationships serve your emotional well-being. When we empower ourselves through awareness, reflection, and support, we can reclaim our agency and foster healthier connections.

Ultimately, recognizing manipulation serves as the first step toward liberation. When you become adept at identifying those behaviours, you gain the ability to navigate your coexistence with clarity and confidence. Grounded in a deeper understanding of both yourself and your relationships, you can strive toward fostering connections built on mutual respect, trust, and love.

In the end, we can choose to relinquish control to unhealthy dynamics or choose to empower ourselves, becoming advocates for our emotional security and well-being. Recognizing manipulation is not just a defensive manoeuvre; it is an act of self-love and an essential step toward building fulfilling relationships that celebrate our authenticity and nurture our growth.

Establishing Healthy Boundaries

Establishing healthy boundaries in our relationships is vital to ensuring that our interactions are respectful, equitable, and conducive to our mental well-being. In the context of manipulation and control, boundaries act as protective barriers that allow us to maintain our sense of self while navigating connections with others. When we lack boundaries, we become vulnerable to emotional exploitation and power plays, often sacrificing our needs and desires to appease others. Therefore, understanding how to set and maintain these boundaries is crucial for any individual seeking to reclaim their autonomy and foster healthier relationships.

We Are Our Own Enemies

To begin with, it is essential to recognize the underlying dynamics that fuel manipulation. Manipulative behaviours often stem from a desire for control, an impulse to maintain power over others. Whether these behaviours are overt or subtle, they often manifest in ways that attempt to undermine our self-esteem, disregard our feelings, or push our boundaries. It becomes imperative to counter these dynamics by advocating for ourselves through the establishment of clear, respectful boundaries. First, we must engage in self-reflection to identify the limits we want to set. This process involves understanding our values and recognizing our emotional triggers. What makes us uncomfortable? What behaviours do we find unacceptable? By taking the time to understand our unique needs, we can articulate our boundaries more effectively.

One effective strategy for identifying these boundaries is journaling. Writing down our thoughts and feelings can reveal patterns and highlight specific areas where we feel disrespected or manipulated. This exploration allows us to gain clarity about our needs and the specific limits we wish to set in various relationships. For instance, if a friend consistently interrupts us during conversations, we may recognize that we need to establish a boundary regarding how we communicate with one another. Once we have identified our boundaries, the next step is to communicate them clearly. Assertive communication is crucial in this process. Assertiveness is not the same as aggression; it is about expressing ourselves confidently without undermining others. Using "I" statements can be particularly effective, as they centre the message around our feelings rather than placing blame. For example, instead of saying, "You always interrupt me," we can rephrase it to, "I feel overlooked when I'm interrupted while speaking." This kind of language conveys our emotions without provoking defensiveness in the other person.

When discussing our boundaries, timing, and preparedness are key. Choose a moment when both parties are calm, and emotions are not running high. Approach the conversation with an open mind, ready to listen as much as you are to share. A constructive dialogue can lead to greater mutual understanding and respect, and may even prompt the other person to examine their own boundaries.

Another essential aspect of establishing healthy boundaries is consistency. Once we communicate our limits, we need to uphold them. This consistency not only reinforces our intentions but also signals to those around us that our boundaries are non-negotiable. Violations should be addressed immediately. If someone crosses a boundary we've set, it's essential to speak up rather than let feelings of resentment fester. Ignoring the issue can lead to feelings of powerlessness and reinforce the belief that our needs do not matter. When addressing boundary violations, it can be beneficial to employ assertive communication techniques again. Use the same "I" statements to express how the violation affected you and remind the other person of the boundaries you've set. For instance, if someone disregards your request for personal space, you might say, "I've mentioned that I need some personal space, and I felt uncomfortable when you continued to invade that space." This reinforces the importance of the boundary and emphasizes its significance to our well-being.

In addition to clear communication and consistency, it is equally important to be prepared for resistance or pushback. Some individuals may react negatively to boundaries because they feel challenged or threatened by the change. This response can manifest as guilt-tripping, anger, or manipulation to regain control. It is crucial to stand firm and remember that boundaries are a healthy and necessary component of relationships. Recognizing that defensive reactions often stem from their discomfort can help de-personalize their responses, allowing us to remain focused on our needs.

Moreover, it is essential to practice self-compassion during this process. Setting boundaries can feel uncomfortable, especially if we're not used to asserting ourselves. We may worry about coming off as rude or uncaring, but advocating for our well-being is a fundamental form of self-respect. Remind ourselves that we have a right to define what is acceptable in our lives and relationships. Engaging in positive self-talk and acknowledging our courage to establish boundaries can help bolster our resolve, making it easier to articulate and maintain them over time.

Another practical strategy for establishing boundaries is to involve others in the process when appropriate. Seeking support from friends or therapists can provide us with external perspectives and encouragement. These individuals can help us rehearse difficult conversations and offer support when boundaries are tested. Additionally, sharing our journey can cultivate accountability and reinforce our commitment to maintaining healthy limits. Additionally, using visual aids can serve as a powerful reminder of the boundaries we've established. Post-it notes with affirmations or descriptions of our limits can be placed strategically in our living or working environments to remind us of our commitment to ourselves. These visual cues can help reinforce the idea that we are in charge of our lives and that our needs are valid.

Furthermore, boundaries are not only about repelling negative behaviours; they can also be about inviting positive behaviours into our lives. For example, we can establish boundaries regarding how we allow others to support us emotionally. In a supportive relationship, openly communicating what kind of help we appreciate can foster a more nurturing connection. This not only enhances mutual respect but also empowers the other person to invest in the relationship in a meaningful way.

It is also essential to recognize that boundaries can change over time. As we grow and evolve, our needs and limits can shift. It is crucial to remain adaptable and reassess our boundaries periodically. Communication should be ongoing, and we should feel comfortable revisiting discussions about boundaries as new situations arise. A dynamic approach ensures that our relationships remain healthy and that they adapt to our changing needs.

Lastly, there is a profound need to explore the boundaries we set with ourselves. Self-boundaries are just as important as those we establish with others. This includes recognizing and adhering to our limits regarding the tasks we take on, the commitments we make, and how we treat ourselves emotionally and physically. Practicing self-care, respecting our time, and saying "no" to unrealistic expectations contribute to healthier self-boundaries. In conclusion, establishing healthy boundaries is a vital practice for safeguarding ourselves against manipulation and control. This process requires self-reflection, assertive communication, consistency, and a willingness to stand firm despite potential resistance. By focusing on our needs and articulating them clearly, we empower ourselves to foster healthier relationships. In navigating the complexity of human interactions, let us remember that boundaries are not barriers; they are gateways to more profound respect, understanding, and connection. By advocating for ourselves, we become not only guardians of our own hearts but also catapults for growth within our relationships. With the right tools and support, we can shift from a place of vulnerability to one of strength, creating spaces where empathy and understanding flourish. Ultimately, as we learn to

We Are Our Own Enemies

establish and maintain our boundaries, we take a crucial step toward transforming our lives and relationships into those that are harmonious and mutually supportive.

Greed: The Root of Many Evils

The Allure of Greed

In a bustling city where skyscrapers met the horizon and the hum of life echoed through the streets, The Seeker wandered through the throngs of people, each caught in the rhythm of a pursuit. It was not the pursuit of happiness, but rather an insatiable chase for more—more power, more recognition, more possessions. To The Seeker, the city was a living organism, responding to its inhabitants' insatiable greed as though it were an infection that had spread through its veins. The Seeker observed families filling their shopping carts with lavish brands, their eyes glossed over with a lust for the next best thing. Each product flashed tantalizingly across billboards like forbidden fruit, promising fulfilment but delivering only momentary satisfaction. Glassy-eyed consumers sprinted from store to store, fuelled by the crass connection between self-worth and material accumulation. The more they consumed, the emptier they seemed. The Seeker leaned against a lamppost, watching as a father scolded his child for merely asking for a new toy. The child's small face fell, not just from the reprimand, but from the realization that what should have been a joyful outing was now a painful reminder of their father's priorities. In this moment, The Seeker saw the first ripple of greed's effects—disconnection in the very fabric of familial bonds.

As the day turned to dusk, the Seeker wandered further, pulling thoughts from the jaws of observation. An old café, tucked away from the bustling crowds, beckoned him with its aroma of freshly brewed coffee. Inside, an elderly woman sat alone at a corner table, leafing through a worn magazine. A thick scarf, frayed around the edges, hugged her shoulders, and her fingers lingered over a crinkled

We Are Our Own Enemies

advertisement showcasing a luxurious cruise. The Seeker couldn't help but notice the longing etched across her face—a longing not so much for the cruise itself but for the experiences it promised, a life she felt she had missed in the shadows of necessary sacrifices.

As the woman's thoughts dissolved into reverie, The Seeker was reminded that greed was not simply about material possessions; it was woven into the fabric of missed moments and opportunities. The drive for more seeped into every aspect of life, often resulting in a pursuit of the unattainable. Every lavish advertisement drew a blueprint for happiness in the guise of wealth and success, selling dreams that could never be fully realized. The Seeker left the café, the woman's reflection etched in his mind—a poignant illustration of how greed shapes our perspectives of happiness and success.

He continued, his thoughts drifting to the workplace—a microcosm where ambition often mingled with greed. As The Seeker stepped into a nearby corporate building, he was met with the familiar sound of clattering keyboards and hushed conversations. Here, the relentless drive to climb the corporate ladder disguised itself as ambition. Colleagues smiled warmly at one another, yet the glint in their eyes told an entirely different story. Each seemed to engage in a silent competition hidden beneath a veneer of camaraderie.

In this world, promotions were not only coveted; they were prizes in a game where the rules shifted to reward those who played with sharp elbows and questionable ethics. The Seeker witnessed a manager thanking his team for their hard work, but it was all a cover for his intent to take credit for their ideas. In the corner of the room, a woman quietly lamented not being recognized for her contributions to a significant project; the fear of being outmanoeuvred weighed heavily on her. The Seeker caught fleeting glances of frustration and resentment, emotions simmering just beneath the surface. This office—a space originally designed for collaboration—had transformed into a battlefield, each individual pitted against the other, fuelled by envy and greed.

With each step The Seeker took through the city, he began to feel the weight of this insatiable greed—not only as a mass phenomenon but as a deeply personal experience. He sensed how greed had torn apart communities, disintegrated trust, and sparked discord among diverse groups. Neighbours turned into strangers as ambitions grew at the expense of kindness. Charity events, once filled with heartfelt intentions, had become showcases for personal branding—opportunities to flaunt wealth rather than extend compassion.

These observations coalesced in The Seeker's mind into a simple truth: greed obscures genuine happiness and fulfilment. It pressures us to reframe our values, transforming our understanding of self-worth into a warped equation of material accumulation. The simple joys of life—connection, love, and shared experiences—are swept aside under greed's insistent demands. He considered how cultures categorized success, trailing the threads of social narrative related to wealth, fame, and possession. Many individuals subconsciously adopted these ideals, equating their self-worth with their net worth. Would they ever find enough, or was an endless pursuit their fate?

As night deepened, The Seeker found himself drawn towards a park—an oasis amid the urban sprawl. He took a seat on a bench, observing a group of children playing tag, unencumbered by the burdens of societal expectations. They ran with wild abandon, joy evident in their laughter, blissfully indulging in the simplicity of the moment. Despite their rudimentary games, there was wealth in their shared innocence, a purity untouched by the corruption of greed. Watching them, he pondered how society's relentless chase for more could distort these early lessons in joy and connection.

Yet, he also recognized that the insidious seeds of greed were often sown in childhood through the constant bombardment of idealized images, leading to unrealistic expectations. The toys, the gadgets, the social media portrayals of ideal lives planted imperceptible doubts in young hearts. They learned that being enough depended on possessing more and sharing less, a false narrative that set the stage for discontent that would carry into adulthood.

As The Seeker surveyed the greens sprawling in front of him, he could hear the echoes of gentle conversations. An elderly man sat nearby, his eyes twinkling as he shared a chuckle with his wife over a shared memory, completely oblivious to the world outside their bubble. Their laughter interrupted the pervasive silence, a reminder of what life should be about: connection, joy, and the momentary flicker of happiness that comes from being present with one another. This was a stark contrast to the performance of greed, where happiness is contingent upon external validation.

How often had he himself succumbed to benchmarking happiness against external standards? He recalled moments of false triumph, standing on a corporate pedestal only to find the view lacking vibrancy, as hollow as the accolades themselves. Then, there were fleeting flashes of joy ignited by genuine connections—an act of kindness, a word of encouragement, or simply the warmth of sharing time with loved ones.

As The Seeker continued to reflect, he observed a group of adults nearby, engaging in an animated discussion about stocks and investments. Their fervour for capital growth felt misplaced amidst the gentle tranquillity of the park, yet it resonated—a competing call of greed that placed wealth over well-being. The conversation was peppered with euphoric chatter about dollar signs rather than the contentment they could cultivate in moments shared with loved ones. The Seeker's heart ached for the lost essence of living—a balance between aspiration and the conscious choice to nurture meaningful relationships.

This dance of opposites—the childlike wonder of play and the oppressive weight of greed—jostled in The Seeker's thoughts. Greed was an alluring spectre, promising unattainable treasures and sparkling futures, yet failing to deliver the very essence of life it promised. The more one sought fulfilment through greed, the more one unwittingly chained oneself to an endless cycle of yearning and dissatisfaction.

With dawn creeping on the horizon, The Seeker's mind continued its tirade against greed. The reflections on consumer culture had propelled an urgent urge for personal examination. How often had he acquiesced to materialism? Had he sacrificed moments of joy for an endless pursuit of success and accolades? The Seeker pondered the implications of aligning his own life with values that fostered greed.

He envisioned a different world—one where individuals rooted their motivations in compassion and integrity rather than hollow desires. Could society shift its narrative? Imagine communities formed by connections that prioritized integrity over acquisition, where self-worth derived from contributions rather than possessions, where ethical living served as a guiding principle. The Seeker lingered over each possibility, clutching them tenderly in his thoughts.

We Are Our Own Enemies

Over time, reflection deepened into action. The Seeker felt an urgent need to step beyond passive observation—an impulse to be a catalyst for change within himself first, and then his community. He began by connecting with those around him, consciously dismissing societal moulds that dictated they were only as good as their possessions. Small gestures became important: offering kindness instead of competition, sharing insights instead of secrets, and finding happiness in simple moments.

As the sun rose higher in the sky, the Seeker found inspiration blooming. People had the power to reshape societal behaviours, to redefine the allure of greed with the strength of shared human experiences. This realization ignited a fire within him—a passion to inspire others to reflect and to realign values from mere consumption towards the appreciation of relationships.

In doing so, perhaps society could slowly begin to unravel a tightly woven tapestry of greed, transforming it into a more compassionate narrative woven from genuine kindness. The risk? It was necessary to embrace vulnerability and authenticity. But the reward? An enriched life filled not with fleeting moments of pleasure but lasting connections and shared happiness.

As The Seeker pondered these thoughts, he recognized the power of collective action. Change could burgeon when individuals joined together in a common cause. Efforts needed to be taken not just for personal enlightenment but to influence cultural attitudes—from consumerism to ethical living. A new way of creating value emerged—one that measured the worth of success by making meaningful contributions, fostering compassion, and prioritizing joy.

In the tapestry of life, it soon became clear to The Seeker that greed, enticing as it may seem, was ultimately a mirage—deceptive and ungraspable. Instead of chasing happiness through material pursuits, perhaps it was wiser to unravel the illusion and focus on nourishing true connections—both to oneself and those around us. This transformation was not merely an internal conflict but a collective evolution from individualistic desires towards a shared humanity.

The Seeker stood, feeling a sense of purpose strengthening within him. There would be challenges along the way, moments of fear and doubt, but the vision for a life redefined—rooted in connection rather than greed—was worth pursuing. One step at a time, the momentum of change could transform not only personal lives but also touch communities and ultimately the larger society.

As he walked away from the park, The Seeker was not just an observer anymore. He envisioned engaging in dialogues, creating spaces for others to reflect on their own relationship with greed, and challenging prevailing norms. His journey marked the beginning, calling others to rise from the hypnosis of consumption to the liberation found in authentic relationships and shared experiences—a quest to reclaim joy, purpose, and ultimately, humanity.

In this pivotal moment, The Seeker not only recognized the allure of greed but harnessed the strength within to abandon its clutch. With reflection, action, and unity, he felt a spark of hope anew—a belief that, in time, individual change could lead to a collective awakening. It was a vision worth holding onto, a legacy worth forging—a tangible reminder that true wealth is born not from what we have but from who we are together.

The Cost of Excess

The glittering façade of wealth often conceals a darker truth, one deeply etched into the annals of human history and our daily lives—

the cost of excess is steep, both in terms of personal fulfilment and societal stability. Greed, the insatiable desire for more, manifests not only in the unyielding accumulation of material possessions but also in the spiritual vacuity it fosters. As we delve into the consequences of greed, we will explore personal accounts that illuminate the profound impact on individual lives and historical narratives that reveal how this vice has shaped the course of civilizations.

Consider the story of Simon, a middle-aged executive in a thriving technology firm. He was originally drawn to the industry out of a genuine passion for innovation and a desire to make a difference. Simon invested long hours and boundless energy into his work, delighted when his ideas began to yield success. However, as profits surged, so did his ambitions. The notion of success twisted, morphing from a measure of personal achievement to an insatiable thirst for power and wealth. Simon began to sacrifice not just his health but also his relationships. Friends grew distant, family gatherings became infrequent, and his once-flourishing marriage dissolved under the weight of his relentless ambition.

As the years passed, something within him began to fray. Wealth had accumulated, but it hardly satisfied. Instead, he felt a gnawing emptiness where once there had been joy. The accolades grew stale, and the bright future he envisioned morphed into an unfathomable void. Ultimately, after reaching the peak of his career, Simon found himself sitting alone in a lavish office, staring blankly at the horizon. Success had imprisoned him in solitude, a poignant reminder of the high cost of his insatiable greed.

Simon's story is not unique; it resonates across cultures and ages, suggesting a universal truth: the rabbit hole of greed has a way of leading its pursuers into a labyrinth from which few emerge unscathed. From personal vignettes to grand historical arcs, the patterns of excess reveal a stark reality: greed often heralds destruction.

In the historical context, we can look back to Ancient Rome, a civilization renowned for its engineering marvels and cultural achievements. Yet, beneath the opulence lay a society deeply marred by greed. An insatiable appetite for wealth and resources drove the expansionist agenda that propelled Rome's dominance. Conquests were not merely acts of military strategy; they were motivated by a longing for riches—gold, lands, and slaves. As a result, Rome expanded its territories to the detriment of many subjugated peoples. The relentless pursuit of wealth not only led to the enslavement and suffering of countless individuals but also sowed seeds of resentment and rebellion within conquered lands.

Moreover, as Rome grew prosperous, societal inequality intensified. The gap between the wealthy elite and the impoverished masses widened, leading to social unrest and political strife. The Roman populace, subjected to hunger and despair, revolted against the very structure that had once promised prosperity. In many ways, the decline of Rome can be traced back to the pernicious effects of greed—a civilization that had sought to elevate itself but ultimately crumbled under the weight of its excesses.

Fast forward to the 17th century, and we encounter a different kind of excess—a time when the desire for wealth and power drove nations to the brink. The Age of Colonialism saw European powers expand their empires in search of new markets, lands, and wealth. The insatiable hunger for resources led to the exploitation of indigenous populations, the destruction of ecosystems, and the establishment of a commerce that respected neither humanity nor the environment. The greed inherent in colonial ventures was not merely a consequence of individual ambition; it was a systemic vice embedded in the very fabric of society.

Take the example of the British East India Company, which played a pivotal role in the colonization of India. As it sought to monopolize trade, it wreaked havoc on local economies and cultures. Greed, cloaked in the guise of economic opportunity, devastated vast communities and altered cultural trajectories. The desire for wealth was so overwhelming that it overshadowed the moral implications of exploitation, resulting in mass suffering and societal disruption.

Historical accounts serve as mirrors reflecting our own experiences. As individuals, we often navigate our lives with aspirations similar to those of great empires—ambition can inspire, but when unchecked, it leads down a treacherous path. Consider the case of Jared, an ambitious entrepreneur who initially built his start-up on principles of social good. Yet, as funding became necessary, he found himself making choices that aligned more with profit than purpose. To cut costs, he hired temporary workers, paid them significantly less, and compromised product quality for a better margin.

Initially celebrated for his vision, Jared's company quickly became a symbol of exploitation, prioritizing profit over integrity. The excess riches gained through shortcuts did not translate into the impact he once envisioned. Instead, his reputation soured, and loyal customers turned away upon discovering the truth about the company's practices. A few years later, Jared was left grappling with a tarnished image and an empty sense of accomplishment, pondering how the pursuit of profit had eclipsed the values he once cherished.

Examining such cases highlights a pivotal truth: greed doesn't merely result in lost relationships or compromised integrity; it presents a formidable barrier to an individual's ultimate fulfilment. When the drive for acquisition supplants values of compassion and community, a profound dissonance arises, breeding a cycle of diminishing returns. The legacy of greed always appears as a mirage—a shimmering promise of satisfaction that evaporates upon reaching out to grasp it.

Furthermore, the ramifications extend beyond the individual into the collective psyche. In societies built upon greed, systemic inequities and injustices proliferate, leading to widespread discontent. The relentless pursuit of wealth translates not only into environmental degradation but also into social policies that favour accumulation over equity. This results in fractured communities, where the wealthy flourish while the impoverished languish, locked in a cycle of despair.

Historical events like the Great Depression underscore this dynamic. The 1920s' unbridled exuberance, fuelled by rampant speculation and a self-serving financial system, ultimately precipitated the collapse of economies worldwide. Greed among institutions, compounded by a disregard for ethical standards, created a volatile atmosphere. The fallout left millions destitute, showcasing that when greed permeates a society's foundation, the consequences ripple outward, ensnaring those who had played no part in the misguided pursuits of wealth.

Transitioning into the present, we witness the haunting spectre of greed manifest in current global crises. The climate emergency, exacerbated by short-sighted policies favouring profit, demonstrates how the pursuit of economic gain jeopardizes the planet's health. Multinational corporations often prioritize shareholder returns over sustainability, contributing to the degradation of ecosystems that future generations depend on. The excesses of capitalism reveal a societal paradox—an economy driven by consumerism breeds a reality where the pursuit of individual success undermines collective well-being.

The environmental degradation resulting from corporate greed elicits profound consequences, affecting not just ecosystems but also vulnerable communities worldwide. Low-income populations often bear the brunt of environmental catastrophes, experiencing the ramifications of pollution, resource extraction, and climate-related crises. Here, greed's destructive impact spirals infinitely, intertwining economic motives with ethical considerations, ultimately revealing the interconnectedness of human lives and the world we share.

Needless to say, the consequences of greed permeate our collective experience, reminding us that the pursuit of excess often yields long-lasting repercussions. As illustrated throughout history, from the decline of great empires to the environmental crises of today, the costs are both personal and communal. Each story of individual struggle echoes a larger narrative about societal integrity and responsibility—a reminder of our shared humanity.

In our quest for insight and growth, it is crucial to grapple with the realities of greed. While the allure of excess may seem innocuous initially, its patterns reveal a darker trajectory, one marked by disillusionment and strife. How, then, do we pivot from these entrenched narratives? How do we redefine success in ways that honour integrity, foster community, and nurture sustainability?

The journey begins with introspection. Reflection allows individuals and societies to confront their desires and motivations. Instead of asking, "What can I gain?" we must shift our focus to "What can I contribute?" By fostering a sense of connectedness to others and recognizing the implications of our choices, we cultivate a healthier society, less influenced by the grip of greed.

Communities can take action by prioritizing social responsibility, encouraging ethical practices, and investing in sustainable solutions. By supporting businesses that value integrity over profit, we contribute to a culture of accountability, diminishing the power of greed. The antidote lies not merely in awareness but also in intentionality, as we define success in terms that enrich lives rather than lining pockets.

Ultimately, the cost of excess is a reminder of the delicate balance between ambition and morality. Greed, with its alluring promise of success, can lead us toward isolated expeditions of self-interest. Yet through personal accountability and collective responsibility, we can redefine our path—a journey towards authentic fulfilment, rooted in compassion, connection, and a shared commitment to a greater good. The choice lies with us; will we let greed dictate our course, or will we forge a new legacy, embracing purpose over profit and unity over division? In acknowledging the costs, we hold the power to sculpt a different future, free from the grip of excess and rich in possibility.

Cultivating Contentment

Cultivating contentment is an art often buried beneath the weight of consumerism and the relentless pursuit of more. In today's world, where the clamour for wealth and status dominates our lives, shifting our focus to gratitude and appreciation can feel revolutionary. The antidote to greed lies not in greater accumulation but in deeper recognition of what we already possess and the connections we nurture. This subchapter will explore methods to foster contentment as a means to combat greed, emphasizing self-reflection and strategies to embrace simplicity.

We Are Our Own Enemies

At its core, contentment emerges from gratitude—an acknowledgment of the blessings that exist in our lives. However, the practice of gratitude is often misunderstood as a passive experience, a fleeting acknowledgment of good fortune without deeper integration into daily life. In reality, gratitude can be an active, transformative force, requiring a conscious effort to engage with the world around us thoughtfully. By cultivating a spirit of thankfulness, we naturally begin to appreciate simple pleasures and meaningful connections. In contrast, greed thrives in an environment devoid of gratitude. When we focus solely on what we lack, envy takes root and distorts our perceptions, perpetuating a cycle of desire that leaves us perpetually unsatisfied.

To start on the journey of cultivating contentment, we must first engage in self-reflection. Taking a step back to examine our motivations and desires is essential. Set aside a few quiet moments each day, whether in the morning or before bed, to journal about your feelings. What do you feel grateful for today? Is it a conversation with a friend, a beautiful sunset, or perhaps a comforting meal? By documenting these moments, you shift from a scarcity mindset, consumed by what you do not have, to an abundance mindset, recognizing the richness of your daily experiences.

In addition to journaling, mindfulness practices serve as powerful tools for cultivating contentment. Mindfulness invites us to be present, allowing us to embrace the here and now rather than getting lost in thoughts of the future or past. Engage in mindfulness meditation for just a few minutes each day. Sit comfortably, close your eyes, and focus on your breath. Inhaling and exhaling, allow distractions to fade away as you bring your awareness to the sensations of the present moment. As thoughts arise—perhaps thoughts of wanting more—acknowledge them without judgment and gently bring your focus back to your breath. This simple practice can foster a profound sense of peace and openness, enabling you to appreciate the present for what it is rather than longing for something more.

Another practice to consider involves creating a gratitude jar. Find a simple container and fill it with slips of paper on which you write down moments, experiences, or people for whom you feel grateful. Make it a habit to add to the jar every week. Over time, this physical representation of gratitude will serve as a reminder of the wealth already present in your life, encouraging you to shift your focus away from consumerist desires to the beauty of meaningful relationships and experiences. On days when you feel overwhelmed by the pressures of your ambitions or tempted by envy, you can revisit the jar, each piece of paper a testament to the richness of your life.

Moreover, embracing simplicity itself is fundamental to cultivating contentment. In a world inundated with messages that equate happiness with accumulation, simplifying our lives can liberate us from unnecessary burdens. Consider decluttering your physical space by donating items you no longer need or use. Each item released provides not only physical space but also emotional clarity. By removing distractions rooted in materialism, you create a sanctuary where gratitude can thrive.

Simplicity can also extend beyond physical possessions to our routines and commitments. Assess where you spend your time and energy. Are there activities or obligations that drain your spirit? Intentional simplicity may involve saying no to commitments that don't align with your values or bring you joy, allowing you to better focus on relationships and experiences that truly matter. By embracing a simpler lifestyle, you create room for genuine connections, whether through shared meals, exploring nature, or engaging in meaningful conversations.

Nurturing contentment also requires us to redefine success. In a society that often measures worth by wealth, the ability to reframe our understanding of success can have a profound impact. Create your own definition of success based not on material gains but on fulfilment, connections, and personal growth. Reflect on what truly brings you joy and contentment. This could involve finding a passion project, connecting with loved ones, or simply taking the time to enjoy the beauty around you. By aligning your pursuits with personal values, you'll be less susceptible to the lure of greed.

In cultivating contentment, it is essential to acknowledge the power of connections. Meaningful relationships can act as the antidote to greed, offering joy and fulfilment that material possessions fail to replicate. Take the time to deepen your connections with others. Schedule regular catch-up sessions with friends, plan family gatherings, or volunteer in your community. These interactions foster a sense of belonging, reminding us that we are part of something greater than ourselves.

As you engage with others, practice active listening. Giving others your full attention can transform interactions from mere exchanges of words into deep, meaningful conversations. When we listen intently, we not only honour the individuals we are with but also cultivate greater appreciation for their experiences and perspectives. This mindfulness in our relationships creates a supportive environment where gratitude can flourish.

In line with nurturing gratitude and connection, consider the practice of random acts of kindness. Small gestures, whether writing a kind note to a colleague or surprising a friend with coffee, can significantly brighten someone's day—and yours. Acts of kindness remind us of the interconnectedness of humanity, reinforcing the perspective that joy and abundance come not just from what we accumulate but from bringing light to others' lives.

Furthermore, the significance of self-compassion must not be underestimated. We often fall prey to comparison and self-judgment, particularly in a society where social media showcases lives curated to appear perfect. Recognize that everyone faces struggles and that it is human to desire more at times. Rather than criticizing yourself for not having as much as someone else, practice self-kindness. Acknowledge your emotions without judgment and remind yourself that your worth does not hinge on material success. By infusing your inner dialogue with compassion, you cultivate a sense of self-acceptance that dampens the fires of greed.

As essential as individual practices are, it is vital to engage in collective efforts aimed at fostering contentment. Community initiatives that promote shared experiences and support systems offer a powerful counterbalance to materialistic pursuits. Look for opportunities in your community that emphasize collaboration and unity. Whether it involves participating in local events, supporting local businesses, or joining community service activities, engage actively in efforts that celebrate shared values over personal gain. Establishing a greater sense of community cultivates gratitude not only for our successes but also for the collective spirit that binds us together.

Moreover, we can look to the global community for inspiration. Throughout history, people have found contentment in mutual support and collaboration, often in the face of adversity. Traditions rooted in gratitude exist globally and can serve as models for cultivating contentment in our own lives. Consider incorporating cultural practices that celebrate abundance, such as sharing meals or

We Are Our Own Enemies

exchanging handmade gifts. These rituals remind us that true wealth lies not in individual acquisition but in community sharing and the bonds we build.

Ultimately, the journey toward cultivating contentment is driven by choice. Commit to shifting your perspective systematically, day by day, and moment by moment. Transform each encounter into an opportunity for gratitude. Allow appreciation for simplicity and connection to replace the hollowness of greed. Recognize that contentment is not a destination but a continuous journey that invites you to find joy in what you have rather than in what you want.

As we progress through life, the challenges of being enticed by greed will inevitably persist, as will societal pressures to conform to a narrative of accumulation. However, the antidote lies within ourselves. By embracing gratitude, nurturing connections, and simplifying our lives, we can dismantle the hold that greed has over our happiness. In doing so, we cultivate a deep sense of contentment that allows us to break the cycle of dissatisfaction, reorienting our grateful hearts toward an abundance that flourishes within and beyond ourselves.

As you embark on this journey, remember that every effort counts, no matter how small. Take heart in knowing that you are not alone in this pursuit. We are in this together, creating a world where the roots of greed can be uprooted and the seeds of gratitude and contentment will flourish. By practicing self-reflection, nurturing relationships, simplifying our lives, and committing to kindness, we choose a more fulfilled existence defined not by what we possess but by the richness of our experiences and connections to one another. In this commitment, we find the true antidote to greed, transforming our lives and the lives of those around us. Together, we can create a more compassionate world, one rooted in love and contentment, where greed is a fleeting memory rather than a permanent fixture.

Foreword

We Are Our Own Enemies is more than just a collection of words on paper; it is a mirror, a challenge, and an invitation. It asks us to look within, to confront the battles we so often create for ourselves, and to rediscover the power of choice, resilience, and self-awareness.

As you open these pages, I want to pause first and thank you. Thank you, remarkable reader, for choosing to embark on this journey with me. In a world overflowing with noise, distractions, and fleeting moments, you chose to lend me your most valuable gift—your time. For that, I am deeply grateful.

This book was written with you in mind: the thinker, the dreamer, the seeker of truth. I hope that within these chapters, you will not only wrestle with ideas but also recognise echoes of your own life and experiences. May you find both challenge and comfort, questions that stir your spirit, and reflections that encourage growth.

I believe that every story, every struggle, and every lesson carries the potential to transform, not just the one who tells it, but also the one who receives it. In that sense, you are not a passive reader; you are a co-creator of this journey. Your thoughts, your interpretations, and your willingness to reflect breathe life into these words far beyond what I could have imagined alone.

As you move forward, I encourage you to hold onto the sparks ignited here. Let them guide you, question you, and propel you to engage with the world around you more intentionally. Share your story, weave your voice into the larger human narrative, and never forget that even in our struggles, we are never truly alone.

This book closes with gratitude but opens a door to countless new beginnings. So, step boldly into your own story. Question, reflect, grow, and above all, live with purpose.

With deepest appreciation and hope,

Daniel Meguille

www.ingramcontent.com/pod-product-compliance
Lightning Source LLC
Chambersburg PA
CBHW052031070526
44584CB00016B/1991